MEN UNDER CONSTRUCTION

Challenges and Prospects

MURRAY STEIN

CHIRON PUBLICATIONS • ASHEVILLE, NORTH CAROLINA

www.ChironPublications.com

Interior and cover design by Danijela Mijailovic
Printed primarily in the United States of America.

ISBN 978-1-63051-792-2 paperback
ISBN 978-1-63051-793-9 hardcover
ISBN 978-1-63051-794-6 electronic
ISBN 978-1-63051-795-3 limited edition paperback

Library of Congress Cataloging-in-Publication Data

Names: Stein, Murray, 1943- author.
Title: Men under construction : challenges and prospects / Murray Stein.
Description: Asheville : Chiron Publications, 2020. | Includes bibliographical references. | Summary: "Today more than ever men are challenged to take steps toward greater consciousness and psychological development. In these lectures Murray Stein describes five "eras" or stages in a lifelong process of psychological and spiritual growth, as well as speaking about friendship between men and the archetypal gestures of fathering. The lectures are intended to help men of all ages to orient themselves in their lives as they search for meaning and seek personal development. This is a very personal book, made up of three series of lectures Murray Stein gave in the 1980's. Although the times have changed since then, the basic issues have not, and the Zeitgeist remains one of ambiguity about male identity and a man's responsibilities toward himself, his children and the world"— Provided by publisher.
Identifiers: LCCN 2020016277 (print) | LCCN 2020016278 (ebook) | ISBN 9781630517922 (paperback) | ISBN 9781630517939 (hardcover) | ISBN 9781630517946 (ebook)
Subjects: LCSH: Men—Psychology. | Maturation (Psychology) | Interpersonal relations. | Fatherhood—Psychological aspects.
Classification: LCC HQ1090 .S734 2020 (print) | LCC HQ1090 (ebook) | DDC 646.700811—dc23
LC record available at https://lccn.loc.gov/2020016277
LC ebook record available at https://lccn.loc.gov/2020016278

TABLE OF CONTENTS

A Short Preface

My junior high school in Grand Forks, North Dakota, was blessed with an inspirational science teacher with a great sense of humor. We loved her. I don't remember her name, sadly, but recall that she was a tall and sturdily built woman in her 30s who had not married and seemed totally dedicated to her vocation as a teacher. We learned about modern physics and astronomy from her, and she opened our eyes to the wonders of the scientific discoveries of the twentieth century. One day she came into class and told us a story from her weekend. She had been driving down a long and boring highway in North Dakota and decided to take a coffee break. Pulling over into a rest stop she saw a car marked as military with a sign on the back that read: "U.S. Marines. We Build Men." She went into the café, looked around, and saw the Marines from the car. Walking up to them boldly, she called out: "Build me a man!" We all laughed when she told us this story, and for some reason I've never forgotten it.

It raises the question: Do boys naturally grow into mature men, or do such men have to be built? Are men products of nature or of culture? In other words, how much of individuation is an *opus contra naturam*, an artifact of culture and individual will? And what role do the archetypes of the collective unconscious play in masculine development? The answer to this will depend in part on whether one takes archetypes to be a part of human nature or a cultural influence. I lean toward the former but recognize the powerful effects of culture on all human beings, especially in the first half of life.

The stages of male development observed cross-culturally and through historical time seem quite similar. They proceed from infancy and childhood through adolescence and young adulthood to mature adulthood and old age consistently, although in somewhat different renditions due to cultural and geographical factors. The same stages are evident and marked. This argues for inherent nature governing the development from boy to man. However, this patterning of development is always strongly assisted by social and cultural influences and pressures. So, it may be that the Marines do indeed build men (culture), but it must go along the lines of inherent patterns and tendencies (nature) that make this model of a man possible.

Of course, if you argue that archetypal patterns are mainly cultural artifacts and not inherent in human nature, then most features of development are due to culture while nature plays little role. But there is still the physical body, and this is without doubt a contribution of nature and the evolution of the species.

In my view, individuation in both men and women is a complex interweaving of physical, psychological, and cultural factors. How a person develops, matures, in other words individuates, depends on a multifactorial panoply of forces. Each factor contributes to the dynamic process, and each makes an essential contribution to the final result. In the lectures that comprise this volume, I try to give due respect to all of them, but my primary emphasis is on the psychological. I recognize that the individual psyche is by no means independent of the body; it is a part of the culture it inhabits. But too often the psychological is overlooked in favor of physical and cultural factors, and I would like to contribute to a rebalancing of the picture. It is in this spirit that I offer these reflections.

This volume is made up of several sets of lectures given at the C.G. Jung Institute of Chicago in the 1980s and 1990s. I have reviewed the manuscripts and made some minor alterations but chose to leave them mostly as they were delivered at that time. I am keenly aware that postmodern culture has changed the picture of male and female identity formation and development dramatically. In the 1980s, LGBT issues were not widely known, and the gender differences, while somewhat up for review due to challenge of feminism, were still relatively stable. Today, such hard and fast distinctions based on biological sex have liquefied and become fluid. Gender choice is thought among young people to be arbitrary, and gender to be a social construction and not a biological given. Notions of essentials and essences are generally considered retrograde and outmoded. If I were writing these lectures today, I would have to take this cultural situation fully into account. But I don't think I would change my fundamental position. Cultures fluctuate in preferences of style, but the underlying archetypal structure of the individuation process does not change at the same rate, if at all. Even today, most people only observe the fluctuations and proceed to individuate along archetypal lines unconsciously and spontaneously. The basic patterns remain because they are embedded in our inheritance as human beings, in the collective unconscious, and they can be discerned through the mists of cultural fluctuations and styles.

I am grateful for the opportunity provided by Chiron Publications to bring these lectures into the light of day at this particular time because it seems to me more important than ever to have a sense of what is possible in the way of men's development. Too often this is left off at the stage of heroic ego development, with everything else seen as either inadequate or superfluous. I have tried to follow Jung's line of thinking that individuation continues throughout the lifetime of the person and has a goal that lies far beyond what the United States Marine Corps. strives to build.

Lectures on Five Stages of Men's Psychological Development

Introduction

I will be speaking in these lectures about five stages in the psychological development in men. By agreed upon convention in the field of developmental psychology, this process of maturation is arranged in a series of chronological stages. I conform to this usage to describe five phases in a man's development, but to begin I should explain what I mean by "stages."

The general view among non-specialists is that one enters a stage of psychological development at a certain age, takes up the tasks appropriate to that stage, solves them (or not), and then moves on to the next stage. This is perhaps true in a very broad sense in the first half of life and follows, more or less, the observed stages of biological development from infancy to adulthood. But it is misleading as an accurate description for how people grow into themselves over the course of an entire lifetime. Psychological development is messier than that. We don't pass through and leave discrete stages as such, but we do develop—only it's not by opening and closing doors in well-ordered sequential stages. Psychological development, which

I will hereafter refer to also as individuation, goes forward sequentially but in a pattern of cycles. The image of the spiral is closer to the reality we experience and witness than the image of a straightforward passage through chronological eras that move unilaterally in one direction through time. A "stage" is a way of speaking about a period in life when certain issues seem more pressing and prominent than others. A name like "childhood" or "adolescence" becomes attached it. The problem is that we find ourselves engaging the same issues again and again throughout life, and if we are indeed developing, then with each pass we make a little gain in consciousness, or freedom, or integration. But we can be sure that we will pass that way again, over the same ground as before. If we are doing our work, then each passing is a little more conscious, a little deeper, a little truer to the self we are.

Erik Erikson proposed a theory of eight stages of psychosocial development that are evident in the course of a lifetime. Every student of psychology learns these stages by heart. Most famously, Erikson wrote about the stage of identity development that occurs during adolescence. This is typically a turbulent period in people's lives, and sometimes it involves a crisis filled with angst and uncertainty about what kind of person one is ands wants to become. But it is certainly the case that the question of identity plays a role in every transitional period, sometimes with more intensity, sometimes with less. We go through a process of identity formation as small children, and we are engaged in the process of identity formation and reformation in midlife and in old age. Each time the question of identity comes up in our lives, we make a little more progress on it. We might see ourselves more clearly, or simply differently, with new aspects emerging out of the mist, new formations appearing, or with old aspects coming more prominently to the fore. Identity is a work in progress throughout our lives. We never leave the issue of identity behind once and for all. We circumambulate this question as identity changes and expands its scope. It is the same with intimacy, the next stage in Erikson's program. We have to deal with it in childhood and throughout life, not only after adolescence in early adulthood as Erikson positions it. So it is with all the stages on Erikson's list.

When I speak in the following pages of the development of men "out of the mother" and "out of the father" into a relatively free space of choice and relatedness, I am not saying that these developments follow a strictly linear sequence from "a" to "b" to "c" without residues. I am going to insist, rather, that one never completely frees oneself from the mother or from the father, and that there are only relative freedoms from them, and one has to keep working at these issues throughout life. Still, there are important change in one's sense of self and purpose, and development does occur.

Jung's advice on the subject of insoluble developmental problems was that we cannot overcome them directly, we can only outgrow them. I would recommend this strategy: learn to love the insoluble problems of freeing yourself from mother and father, because these problems are worth the time and effort and are worthy of your most careful consideration. You will pass over them innumerable times in the course of your life, each time with more consciousness, seeing more deeply into the implications and dynamics, each time loosening a deeper strand of the limitations these complexes have created. The goal of the development I am going to propose, the *telos* of a man's inner development, is to achieve as much freedom from them as possible, true freedom, in order to release the full panoply of potentials in the self. And the traps and seductions and illusions of freedom along the way toward that freedom are almost infinite.

I look on this work as a statement of vision of what men can become, rather than a research-based social scientific report. Further research is, of course, invited and welcome.

The Five Stages of a Man's Life — A Brief Overview

The diagram below sketches a model of psychological development in a man over the normal lifespan, assuming an achieved age of 80+ years. As it shows, his psychological movement passes through five major periods, or "stages," in the course of the individuation process.[1] This model provides the general framework for discussing the developmental issues and challenges I will be considering in the following lectures.

Stages Of A Man's Life

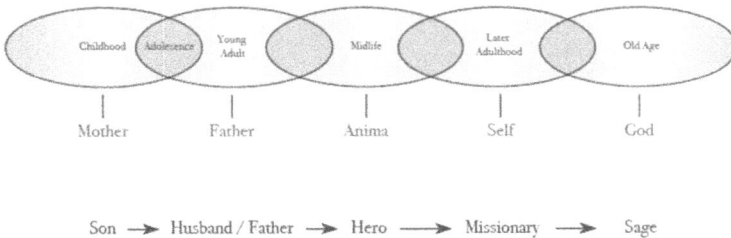

| Childhood | Adolescence | Young Adult | | Midlife | | Later Adulthood | | Old Age |

Mother   Father   Anima   Self   God

Son ➤ Husband / Father ➤ Hero ➤ Missionary ➤ Sage

Diagram #1.

Diagram #1 shows discrete circles that designate stages, but it should additionally be arranged in the form of a spiral as in Diagram #2.

The circles nest inside one another, rising gradually and progressively emerging from one to the other. The transitional areas between the stages are shown in Diagram #1 at the intersection of the

---

[1] I will use the term, "individuation," throughout these lectures to speak of full-lifespan psychological development. It is a term used by Jung to indicate the process of personality development from birth to death.

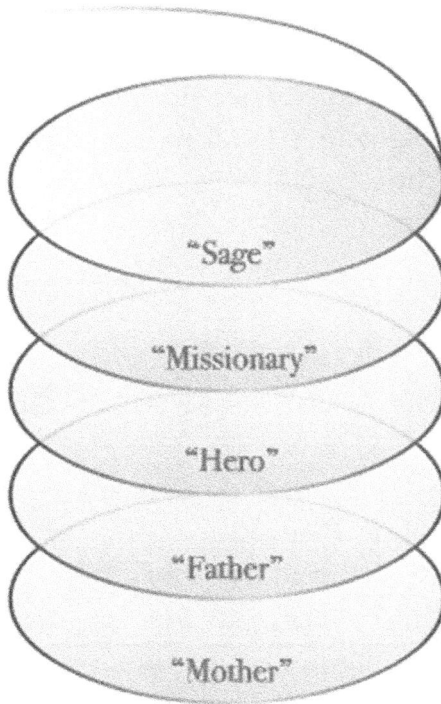

Archetypal Dominants Of
The Life Cycle

Diagram #2.

contiguous circles. The circles and links in the model
are stretched out or condensed in time according to
cultural and other factors such as life expectancy.

I will now give a brief synopsis of each of the
five stages for purposes of orientation. In the lectures
that follow, I will focus on each in turn.

The initial phase of a man's development, which covers infancy and childhood, is dominated by the mother. I refer to this stage as "in the mother," since the child's conscious horizon is more or less enveloped in the atmosphere of the maternal. It is a period of containment and nurturance. The transition from this stage to the next takes place in adolescence, which begins around the age of 12 and lasts until a solid residence has been taken up in the next stage. This is a first step in the lifelong process of separation.

The figure of the father dominates the second stage, and I will speak of it as "in the father." The psychic horizon here is framed by the patriarchal attitude, either personal or cultural. Separation from the second stage and transition to the third stage begins around the age of 35 and lasts until approximately the age of 50. As the maternal dominates the first stage and the patriarchal the second, the soul, or anima, features as the dominant figure in the third stage.

The fourth stage, which lasts roughly from the age of 50 to the mid-70s, concerns the development of the ego-self axis and is characterized by the emergence and increasing consciousness of the self as an important psychic factor. This stage moves gradually, and usually without a major break in consciousness into the fifth and final stage, in which spirituality and the "God problem" enter as the main themes of further individuation. I call this "late stage individuation."

11

Each of the dominant figures in these five stages—Mother, Father, Anima, Self, and God—presents specific typical problems and challenges that have to do with the sense of a man's identity. In stage One, he is "mother's boy." As he frees himself from this stage, he moves on to become "father's son." There may be a formal rite of passage that marks this change in identity. During the second stage, he often becomes a father himself, even while his identity remains that of son of the father. In the midlife stage, there is a further demand for separation from parental figures as his sense of identity shifts to that of the hero, whose task is to rescue his soul, the anima, from domination and extinction by the patriarchal world. His identity as hero is diminished in importance as he moves into later adulthood, which I will designate "missionary" because he now finds a mission in the world, which directs his vision outward beyond himself to embrace collective and cultural issues. This is the era of significant engagement with the world. As he moves into old age, this missionary identity gives way to religious questions of ultimate meaning. His sense of identity shifts to "sage" as he becomes a wisdom figure for others.

As I said earlier, each stage pushes psychic material forward into the others. We carry our past with us even as individuation moves further and deeper into full selfhood.

The First Circle: Mother

The Age of the Boy

This first stage in a man's development, which I will speak of throughout these lectures as the "mother stage," forms a platform for all future psychological developments to come and is extensive and complex, consisting of several phases and sub-phases, many of which may be repeated in various forms in later life. It covers the period of childhood, from birth to teens, in which the mother and "mother-child problems" occupy center stage. Here the male child is "a mother's boy" and, ideally, feels loved and admired by her totally.

I will not go into the details of the several phases of early childhood development (much about this topic exists in the psychological literature) except to mention some issues affecting masculine develop-ment specifically. By "mother," it is important to understand, that I mean more than a single caretaking person. The whole surrounding environment of a child is "the mother," in the sense that it is a containing and nurturing context. The personal mother merely symbolizes this total environment, for better or worse.

In the early years, the first significant person in a man's life is (usually) his own biological mother. She is the first significant "other" with whom a physical as well as psychological relationship is established.

This relationship is often referred to as "attachment," following the name given it in the pioneering work of John Bowlby, and it begins already prenatally.

The infant's first extra-uterine experiences of the world are normally centered on the actual mother and are colored importantly by her reception of the newborn. The quality of this reception lays down over time a critical foundational element in a person's basic attitude toward the world and has lifelong consequences. Erik Erikson names the crucial emotional issue of this phase of psychological development "trust vs. mistrust." If the reception is welcoming, stable, and nurturing, and if the infant is sufficiently healthy and responsive, an attitude of trust develops in the young persona. The infant can relate to the world (here represented by the mother) with feelings of trust. A cordial, welcoming reception will encourage a positive outgoing attitude toward the world, while ambivalence shown in a cool or negative reception may produce or strengthen an already existing tendency toward avoidance of relations with the outside world. In summary, the attitude of the mother toward the infant is generally seen as critically important for the future quality of object relations. The relationship to the world established at this stage of life will play a considerable role throughout a man's life.

While still contained within the "mother world," which typically continues until early adolescence, a boy will show strenuous efforts to develop a separate sense of self and autonomy. A boy's efforts to separate himself from his parental caretakers (the "mothers") begin early on and normally gather considerable energy around the age of two ("the terrible twos"). Then, when the three- or four-year-old boy discovers significant physical differences between himself and his mother, he intensifies the separation process from her on a psychological level with the noted gender difference coming prominently into play. A mother, who of course is well aware of this difference and the coming need of her son to separate from her, may facilitate this process or she may try to hinder it. Ambivalence on her part concerning separation can set the stage for emotional conflicts in the son. Is it OK to leave his mother or not? How far can he stray and still remain attached? On the other hand, an anxious mother, anticipating separation too soon, may begin to take distance too early and leave the boy with a feeling of insecurity and abandonment.

There are some typical problems that arise from the nature of the relationship between a mother and son. I will describe a few that I have observed in my practice. This list is by no means exhaustive, to say the least.

1. The man with an absent mother. I recall the case of a man, "Ben," who was thirty years old when he came into my practice. His mother had been heavily medicated and hospitalized with severe mental illness during his early childhood. At the time I saw him,

he was sexually underdeveloped and had several addictions, mostly around eating and alcohol but also involving excessive fantasizing and daydreaming. Having been a fairly good student in school, he was now studying for the priesthood. This course of study was not going very well due to his inability to stay focused. One of the most striking things I noticed about him was what I felt as his "vacancy." In sessions, he would sit down and almost immediately go into a fugue-like state, staring ahead vacantly and un-responsively, as if in a sort of self-induced hypnotic state. When I asked him about it, he said he was "processing." Sometimes, he said, it was "prayer," because he felt that he was communicating with spiritual beings like saints or angels. In one session, upon going into this state he reported to me that he was having a vision of "Our Lady," the Mother figure honored by multitudes in his church, and he was connected to her by an umbilicus through which "food" was passing into him.

Ben was a man whose mother had been incapable of receiving a child into her care. The image of the archetypal Great Mother came to him as a substitute for the missing personal mother, and She offered food and nurturance to him. The psyche compensates for the absence of a real mother by offering a symbolic one, and the neglected child finds refuge there and remains embedded in the archetypal world until a way can be found to exit from it and enter into relationships with individuals and communities. In contrast to a man who has too strong an attachment to his real mother and stays at home well into his adulthood, this man's difficulty was that he could not form an attachment to his mother because she was not there, and so he became attached to an imaginal surrogate. He remained "in the mother" by projecting this archetypal image on to religious objects and institutions.

2. The man with an ambivalent mother. A man aged 33 came into therapy because he felt completely stuck in his life on every level. While he was constitutionally very creative and artistic, bordering on brilliant, he had been unable to engage with the world in an effective way. He remained cocooned. He could not bring himself to present or sell his paintings. His father had not invited him into his business because of the boy's close tie to his mother and his unsuitability for the rough and tumble life out there in the competitive world of commerce. In his adolescence, the boy had dropped out of school, left home, and started to make his way in life completely on his own. He exhibited behavior similar to Ben's in sessions, including fugue-like states and discomfort and distrust when engaged in dialogue. Deep narcissistic injuries and traumas from childhood were evident in his reactions to others, including myself. His relationship to women was severely stressed: he demanded that a woman be completely virginal, a Madonna, but once

in a relationship he constantly berated her and tried to prove that she was a whore and therefore unworthy of him, which drove her away, of course, and left him living alone again.

His dreams showed that he was "stuck in the mother." In one, he was trapped in a grocery store (a mother image) owned by the Mafia (symbolic of the mother's animus). Finally, his father came to the rescue, providing him with the suggestion to pay the Mafia off in order to escape. Thus, his father offered a way out of the mother trap. The dream father was more active than his actual father had been. To me, this suggested a possibility that his transference to me might provide a way out of his stuck condition. The question was how to pay off his mother's controlling animus and get free of her. In the end, he did not succeed, sadly. I felt badly and regretted that I had been unable to help him in his search for liberation.

In this case, we discovered a mother who allowed her boy infant to form an attachment to her but at the same time harbored a deep hostility to men, typically because she herself had been wounded by them and by the patriarchal bias of society. Most importantly, she had a deeply troubled and conflicted relationship with the boy's father, and this led her to draw her son into a tortured marital drama by making him an ally against the father. Since the child was male, however, she saw him both as ally and enemy. This ambiguity was frightening to the son, since sometimes the mother was too close, threatening incest, and at other times she was distant and murderously rageful. Her unpredictability destabilized him and created turbulence in his relationships, especially with women. The father—designated as enemy—could not help, so the son was trapped in the home with a frighteningly unstable mother. The father was probably envious of the child because he seemed to have gained access to the mother's intimacy while he was locked out, and consequently a negative and hostile relationship developed between father and son. The father rejected him and the mother threatened him. He was stuck between them.

3. The man with the faulty-mirror mother. A 50-year-old professional man who was successful in his profession and married with a family of three children had an enduring problem of being unable to feel himself as a man. When looking at himself naked in the mirror, he could not "see" his penis and had no sense of it. He grew up in a family dominated by a strong-willed mother, and his father was weak by comparison and passive. In his adult years, he dealt with his inability to feel his masculinity by looking intently at other men whom he admired and trying to find in himself the qualities that attracted him. He was trying to find himself in the mirror of these projections. He searched for his masculinity by looking outside of himself. It was a more or less hopeless quest since the

missing qualities inevitably remained "out there" in the other and could not be located within. This often brought on spasms of despair.

A mother will typically mirror her child, looking at him with loving eyes and enjoying him for his being, not for abilities or achievements (which will be the father's role) but simply for what he is, in and of himself. One aspect of his nature that is to be also enjoyed by the mother is his maleness, and her positive mirroring of this will enable a strong development of his masculinity. If the mirror is faulty, however, the mother may enjoy him as an infant, cute and cuddly, but she cannot positively mirror and enjoy his maleness as he grows older. She may ignore or suppress acknowledgement of his sex and his male qualities as they appear in childhood. She thus rejects his masculinity, possibly because of her own difficulties with sexuality in her relationships with men. She may dress the boy as a girl and cast him in the role of a daughter she would have preferred. The father is, again, passive, distant, or missing. The boy will have difficulty identifying with his own masculine parts, even if he has no difficulty identifying with other parts of his personhood such as his intellect.

4. The man with a guilt-and-shame-inducing mother. This type of mother does not neutralize, distort, or deny the masculinity of her son, but rather creates an atmosphere of guilt and shame about

typical masculine traits that her son might display. When typical boy behaviors such as aggressiveness, independence, and explorativeness appear, she reacts negatively, shaming the boy. As a man, if he is primarily attached to her rather than to his father (that is, a "mother's boy"), he may seem to some women to be a paragon of gentleness and goodness—but too good to be true. Women like him, but they do not fall in love with him, lacking as he is in basic masculine qualities. He is still "in the mother," and were he to depart from the mother's injunctions, he would feel terrible guilt. Such a man tends to stay close to the female-dominated home and is often service-oriented in his behavior and career. He cannot be his full masculine self, because he is afraid of his mother punishing disapproval and of shaming looks. This constraint operates subtly, pervading daily behavior as a maternal super-ego.

5. The man with the perfect mother. This mother permits the son to attach to her and gives her son enough nurturance and mirroring to keep him from discovering her negative side. Usually she accomplishes this by encouraging him to project the negative feminine outwardly onto someone else, which produces a split for the son between the good woman (herself) and the bad woman (all others). This son becomes the classically mother-bound son. He sees his mother as totally positive—virginal, pure,

good—and other women as much lesser than his mother—problematic, sexual, witch-like, and so on. Thus he idealizes his mother and denigrates other women, often remaining a bachelor and caring for his widowed mother, or cherishing an ideal memory of her. The father is usually rather inconsequential, weak or absent, or thoroughly denigrated by the perfect mother. The son only sees "her sweetness" and gets trapped in it. He feels he must stay with her and protect her, and he feels guilty about any possible relationship with another woman. Typically, she encourages this sense of responsibility. If he is to marry, she encourages marriage to a weak, un-challenging woman. A classic example of the perfect mother is portrayed in the opera, *Carmen*. Don Jose's mother is allforgiving, meek, and non-sexual, in sharp distinction to Carmen who is her complete, and extremely attractive, opposite.

In contrast to all these problematic mothers is the so-called "good enough" mother. She is not the perfect mother because she gives her son her real self, gradually, at a rate that he can handle. She is devoted to nurturing in the beginning, but in time she weans him, allows some distance, permits him to see her anger, her imperfections, her negative side, in short, to see her more and more as she really is. Secondly, she maintains the strength of the early bonding in an appropriate way, which will stand him in good stead throughout his later development. In this, she fosters his ability to achieve intimacy and trust in relationships especially with women. A man's capacity to be open and intimate generally depends substantially on the development of his trust in women, which is first established in his relationship to the good enough mother. Third, she confers on her son a sense of self-confidence, which he can take with him when he leaves her. The mother is the son's first experience of the world and its reliability or lack thereof. If a man is able later to count on his inner good enough mother, his ego will be well-grounded and his sense of self-worth will enable him to proceed through life with resiliency, confidence, and the ability to relate successfully to the world.

In time, the good enough mother will show her son her negative side, which helps him to separate from her. If the mother remains too one-sidedly positive, there may be an irresistible temptation to stay at home with her. The good enough mother shows her negative side in her weaning of him or "abandoning" him to the father or babysitters, and eventually he understands that he is meant to go into life on his own.

The gift of the good enough mother is that a man can be enough at home in his body and in the world to feel and understand his impulses and instincts. In addition, the good enough mother bestows the confidence that he can meet his needs and gratify his desires with success. Therefore, he will know when he is hungry and can seek something to eat; he will know when he wants and needs intimacy and can seek out a suitable partner; he can feel his anger or sadness and can act on them if necessary; he can be active, even aggressive, when a situation calls for it; he can destroy in order to create. When confronted with the negative features of life, he is able to protect himself through his wits and his own knowledge of the world. This type of mother has enabled him to leave the parental household because he has the basis for self-sustenance.

In an optimal development, a man's sense of self is constellated adequately in the Mother Circle so that he is able to move out of the parental home and into the wider world. He can now enter into the Father Circle, the realm of career, development of skills, and the challenges of society. Here, he can express his ambition. In the next stage, he will need to learn to relate to the expectations and requirements of the prevailing culture, which will bring the father into a position of central importance.

The Second Circle: Father

The Age of the Son

If a mother provides her son with the basis for a solid inner sense of self, a father helps him to discover and relate effectively to the outer world of society. As with the term "mother," I am not speaking here exclusively of the actual father but rather of the "fathers," in general, who appear in a man's life in a variety of figures, such as teachers, ministers, politicians, and other leaders, not all of them necessarily biologically male but definitely of a masculine-patriarchal cast in attitude. The feminine side of the self for a man typically constitutes the quality of his inner life, which covers such matters as his experiences of intimacy and soul, that is, his private and inward subjective space. The masculine side typically takes up the dominant space in his ego and persona. In the persona he shows himself to others as a man: he dresses like a man and he acts like a man in a manner acknowledged and approved by his specific culture. The father, a loving and instructing representative of the masculine principle, functions as a bridge to the outer world and helps him to adapt to society positively and to adjust himself to collective expectations. His father figures guide him in learning how to be a man in the real world of work and taxes.

Mother and father contribute, therefore, fundamental structural strands in a man's psychological genetic makeup. They are essential building blocks of a man's personality structure. Moreover, the autonomous and unconscious mother and father complexes are major psychic energy centers that return to affect consciousness over and over again in a continual and lifelong enactment of his psychological life, behaviorally and attitudinally. Like the *leitmotifs* of a Wagner opera, their influences resurface and thread through all the phases and stages of life. Mother and father exist both as real individuals and as complexes and archetypes, each level contributing emotional and psychological influences on the early years of a man's life and forever after.

At the beginning of life, the mother world constitutes the entire object world to which the infant relates. Inner world and outer world are one, and there is no serious division between subject and object. Jung calls this type of relationship, where subject and object are entangled to the point of identity, "participation mystique" ("mystical participation"). It is the earliest form of object relations. While the father is equally primary in the structural formation of the personality, temporally he arrives on the scene later. His image appears as from out of a mist as a second primary figure in the world of the infant child. The father relationship reaches deep into infancy and is lifelong, just as is the mother relationship, but as a significant figure with meaning, he is introduced slightly later in life. With the arrival of the father, the psyche begins the process of differentiation among objects and between inner and outer. Mother is intimate, familiar, close; father is impersonal, strange, and distant. This is the early picture of psychic experience.

The world, at first whole, gradually becomes differentiated and divided as discrete objects begins to emerge in consciousness, and this evokes a variety of reactions. According to Melanie Klein, a first differentiation is made in infancy between "good" and "bad." She locates this discrimination in the infant's relationship to the mother's two breasts. There is an alternation between "good breast" and "bad breast," one breast being felt as nurturing, warm, and comforting, while the other takes on the quality of being persecutory, poisonous, and attacking. This is the origin of the distinction between good and bad, the earliest work of the differentiating function of consciousness, according to Klein. Jung would not necessarily disagree as he sees ego consciousness gradually emerging from the unconscious in the course of infancy. Klein proposes a rather violent and emotional beginning to psychological life. Later researchers like Daniel Stern have taken a more sanguine view of these first beginnings of conscious awareness of material objects. This phase, however, takes place within the original ouroboric (tightly enclosed) relationship between self and other. It represents the beginnings of a differentiation in the inner world.

A different kind of differentiation is made when the "third," that is, father, is introduced into the mother-infant setting. This is not a differentiation within the mother world but between the mother world and the father world, inner versus outer. The differentiating function of consciousness now begins to create another axis: that between woman and man, feminine and masculine, inner and outer. In the unified world of original wholeness, these features exist only as latent possibilities. The original primordial state of oneness becomes divided between good and bad, and then when the figure of the father is introduced into the infant's world, between inner and outer, between mother and father. This yields a fourfold structure for consciousness, which the child will use for basic orientation: good vs. bad, inner vs. outer. The latter distinction becomes the distinction between fantasy (inner) and reality (outer). This later yields two types of thinking: imagination and directed thinking.

It should be said that these same different-iations occur for both girls and boys, but their development diverges because boys tend to go on to identify with the father and girls with the mother. Through her identification with the mother, a little girl sustains a sense of continuity in her identity and tends to remain more inward, imaginative, and close to her mother, while a little boy experiences a rupture in his world as he parts with his mother and as he tends to move outward into the world to be near his father and toward directed thinking. These are gross generalizations but I believe they cover a large majority of cases.

In optimal male development, or what we could refer to as the highly desirable but elusive "normal" development, a mother introduces her son to his father and creates an atmosphere of inclusion that bring the father into what was the dyadic world of mother and infant. This avoids a split and results in a triadic social structure that can be stable and enduring. Ideally, she presents the father as a positive figure and not as a threat to the intimacy between her and her son. In doing so, she helps her son to idealize his father as a figure of pride and high esteem whose importance casts an aura of value on the family as a whole. This initial idealization is absolutely essential for further development because the son is then able to draw upon his native masculine tendencies by identifying with his father and striving to imitate him, feeling that being like him is a good thing and that mother will be supportive and not feel abandoned, wounded, or critical. Out of this idealization the boy's ambition is born. The son's ability to idealize his father and to strive to be like that ideal, provides a motive for further development of his personality.

Later on, usually in early- to mid-adolescence, the son "outgrows" his personal father, discovering some deficiencies and becoming disillusioned with him. At this point, idealization passes on to other male figures such as teachers, coaches, political leaders, and so on, who seem greater than the father and who represent the son's next step out into the world. Again, ambition is constellated in these idealizations as the boy strives to become like his ideals. The relocation of the son's idealizations helps to release the son from his actual father and his parental nest. He can fly away and test his own wings. The father's role at this point, optimally, is to allow himself to be supplanted as his son's ideal and to understand that it is appropriate for his son to move on. Nietzsche observed that it is the mark of a good teacher that his students outgrow him and that he enjoys their development. It is, likewise, the mark of the good enough father that he can enjoy watching his son outstrip him in some ways.

Having been outgrown at this stage, the father will come back in later life, often at midlife, in the memory, imagination, and dreams of his son. He may have died by this time but in the psyche his continued presence is assured. He returns not as the historical father who has been idealized and outgrown, but as a self figure. The archetypal self becomes personalized in this way, moving from the hidden depths of the unconscious to the concrete memory image. Whereas the self may appear in dreams in abstract form such as stars, circles, squares, numbers, and so on, it now may appear in personalized form in the figure of the father.

The Role of the Father: Initiation

The essential role of the father is to initiate his son into manhood, or at least to assist crucially in the initiation. The father accomplishes the earliest phase of this initiation simply by appearing in the world of the mother and by offering himself as an alternative point of orientation, enabling differentiation between the masculine and the feminine, the outer and the inner. He next offers himself as an object of idealization. Not all fathers find it possible to allow themselves to be idealized, and this refusal creates a deficit in the son's development. Idealization places some pressure on the father to live up to a projection. This pressure, which grows stronger as his son gets older, demands that a man live up to an ideal, which can limit his freedom. In this sense, children can be said to create their parents, although some fathers strongly resist this development. A father may reject such idealizations if there is too great a discrepancy between his own (possibly poor) self-image or his lack of maturity, and the ideal image reflected back by his son. He may feel trapped or caged in.

By idealizing his father, the son separates himself further from his mother (and sisters). He may at this point feel that he is better than they are and assert superiority on the basis of the masculine prowess he shares with the father, becoming grandiose about his fantasies (as dragon slayer or superman, like his dad) and feeling full of himself as a male. The idealization of the father operates at several levels—physical (he is bigger, stronger), cognitive (he is smarter, more capable of doing things), and social (he has a wider circle of friends and colleagues). The idealized father is seen as having great knowledge of the world—he lives "out there," he knows about places outside the home, and he can fix things that mother can't. The son will take note of his father's professional or social position and compare that invidiously with the mother's domestic roles. The son thus builds a positive father complex and identifies with his father's masculine presentation of himself as a man in the world, which then become strengthened as other more feminine parts become recessive and fall away into the unconscious.

Eventually, the father will have to allow himself to become de-idealized. This often occurs suddenly and surprisingly. A word will be said, something will be seen, or the father will disappoint in a certain critical way that the son does not quite understand, and the son will consequently feel disappointment and becomes disillusioned. The father is not as great as he had imagined.

The first step in initiation is, then, identification with an ideal; the second is loss through betrayal of that ideal. In the identification stage, the son learns to claim his phallic power and feel his masculine strength, later connecting this to his creativity and fertility. In the second step of initiation, betrayal, the son is released from bondage to the father. The betrayal is essential to prevent the son from being forever bound in the father. James Hillman in his important paper, "On Betrayal," retells an old Jewish story. A father takes his son to the basement of their house where he tells him to climb up on one basement stair and jump into his father's arms. The son complies, and the father catches him. The father then tells him to repeat the action, this time climbing up two steps. The son climbs, jumps, and is caught. Again, says the father, another step higher; and again the son climbs, jumps, and is caught. This is repeated until the son has climbed quite far up the steps. He jumps once more; but this time the father does not catch him. The son falls and is hurt; he is enraged and astonished. The lesson, says the father, is that this is what life is like; moreover, he, the father, will not always be there to catch his son. Thus, the son is released from dependency on the father by an act or instance of betrayal. That betrayal, of course, must come at the right time; and the son must have the wherewithal to grow from the experience and move on into independence. If it comes too early, or too consistently, a negative father complex will develop and with it an aversion to all paternal authority. But the good enough father is able, at the right moment, to show his negative, untrustworthy side to his son and to allow his son to suffer the consequences. All initiations have an element of risk and possible catastrophe. Without that, it is not a true or effective initiation. The outcome of initiation must be a man's sense of his inner resilience, strength, and reliability to deal with life's trials without collapsing.

The Initiated and the Uninitiated

If I contrast the initiated with the uninitiated man, it should be recognized that no man is totally one or the other. These concepts represent the extreme ends of a spectrum based on the relationship with the father. Nonetheless, in observing men, one can often see a clear difference between those more fully initiated and those who are not.

The initiated man has incorporated the masculine in himself as an *inner* structure. It is a part of his self-definition and feeling of self. He has gone through an initiation process or trial, in which he was challenged and found himself able to identify the masculine in himself—feeling his phallus and its strength as a part of himself, and feeling his strength and prowess as a man. Moreover, he has not become bound in dependency to a particular father figure but can use father figures or strong masculine images as points of reference. He is able to use his literal and his symbolic phallus in his life and can therefore stand his ground against other powerful male figures who challenge him. Able to stand on his own two feet, he can make independent judgments, face authority, and carry authority himself. He is what people call "self-confident." Thus, he can be a father—or a manager or a boss or a leader. He is neither dependent on his mother, from whom his father helped to free him, nor on his father, from whom he is freed through initiation.

The Uninitiated Man

The uninitiated man, in contrast, tends to stand beside or outside the circle of masculine authority, as if not quite pulled out of the mother world into the world of the father. He has difficulty feeling his own phallic power or masculine strength. He has a problem with ambition, exhibiting either too much or too little. Tending to look outside of himself for male power figures to identify with, he seeks to bolster his masculine strength vicariously. Examples can be found in the followers of strong leaders who put themselves in the service of such powerful male figures in order to absorb phallic authority by proximity. Similarly, some seek that authority through identification with a powerful corporation or institution. The uninitiated man cannot idealize his own works and prowess, even if they may be quite exceptional in the eyes of the world.

There are two general types of uninitiated men. One type seeks protection as a follower, ever asking for advice and looking for support from strong men in a constant search for a father figure to hide behind. By contrast, the other type is rebellious against male authority figures, asserting seeming independence that actually is counter-dependence in that it needs the other in order to stand upright. This type is unable to idealize a mentor; he approaches potential father figures negatively, often with anger, or he falls immediately into competition with them. This man ends up a loner. At first glance, he may look initiated, but on closer scrutiny one gets the sense of weakness and lack of inner structure. Often, he is subtly mother-bound, such that if the woman on whom he depends is withdrawn he collapses into addiction or attempts suicide.

In fact, most men are located somewhere along a spectrum of initiation. Initiations take place throughout life, beginning with the classical one in adolescence. Later initiations may come about with the assistance of a mentor in college or graduate school, or of employers and institutions in professional life, or in relationships when they end in betrayal and a break. This lifelong process of initiation takes place in the world of the father. The father is the first initiator. If he lays the groundwork well, his son can experience later idealizations and betrayals in a way that will allow him to grow.

Fathers and Sons

As there are types of mother (see previous lecture), so there are types of father. This sets up specific problems regarding a man's transition out of the mother world into the world of the father.

The Absent Father. A man's adult psyche may show a lacuna where the father image should be. The "father effect" is simply not there. This is a man without an internalized image of a father although he may have some memories of one. But the effect of a father in his psychological development is absent. His actual father may have been physically absent, for instance, off to war or living apart as the result of a divorce, or he may have been a non-functioning father for all intents and purposes although in the household. As a result the son is "rudderless" in adulthood. If he had a good enough mother, we could say he has a strong, tight boat, but he does not know where to go with it; he lacks a sense of direction. The absence of ambition to succeed in this world is derivative of this problem. The father was absent as a figure for the son to idealize so the son will not have experienced ambition to be great and heroic like his father, and later on he misses also the feeling of mastery and accomplishment that result when such ambitions are fulfilled. The sense that accomplishments in the real world are better than fantasy achievements does not arrive in this man's life as an effective means for getting him to make the transition out of the mother world.

In the absence of a good enough father, as with the case of the absence of a good enough mother, the psyche compensates by creating an archetypal image of the missing figure. The resulting "divine" father may be so far removed from everyday life that no modification of the lofty ideal is possible, and the son can thus never hope to achieve any of the ideals symbolized in the image. Arthur Colman refers to such an image as the "Sky Father," a purely symbolic father. The real father, who would have functioned as the carrier for idealization and later for gradual modification of the ideal, is absent.

A "rudderless" man, then, is stuck with the problem that if a task is good enough for him to attempt, it will be too great for him to accomplish—or else the contrary: if the task is something he can accomplish, it is beneath him and not worth the effort. Such a man is not necessarily totally dysfunctional, but he does not live up to his inherent potential.

A son of the "rudderless" father has a similar problem, because his father, though able to have a family, cannot pass on the sense of ambition and direction that he himself lacks. The son of such a father may look promising but may also be rudderless, although less so. As a scholar, for instance, he may stop at a master's degree, though the doctorate would be fully appropriate and within his ability. He has identified with the "rudderless" father, and that identification is unbroken because the rudderless father will not have completed the initiation process for his son. Like his father, he has the underlying problem of grandiosity, low self-esteem, and inability to master the small steps that lead to great achievement.

The Abandoning Father. Though this man has some similarities to the man with no father, there are subtle differences. This father may not physically abandon the child but tends to leave him with the mother. He has difficulty in allowing his son to idealize and identify with him, and so he fails to initiate him into the men's world. This father is often a *puer aeternus* ("eternal boy") himself in that he lives more in a world of possibilities and fantasy than in actualities, more in potential than in actualizing potentials. He is often too busy with his own projects to attend to his son. He is distant and cold and does not expect anything of his son. Part of initiation is the expectation of performance by the son; the father makes demands and shows conditional love (as opposed to the mother's classical unconditional love). His conditions on a son's acceptability, if appropriate to the son's stage of development and ability, provide opportunities for achievement and the experience of mastery by the son. The abandoning father is too uncaring and too casual. He does not care whether the boy gets an A or a C in school; he is uninvolved. He cannot, therefore, be an initiation master, who must care what happens to the boy. He is negligent, possibly an alcoholic. The son of an alcoholic father experiences his father as an abandoning father (and a threatening one if the mother and children are endangered by his drinking), because he is involved in his own addiction and mother-bound problems.

The Oedipal Father. Freud described the father-son relationship in terms of the classic Oedipus complex. In this view, the son comes to occupy a privileged place with the mother, creating jealousy in the father. The father becomes a threat to the son because he wishes to assert his priority with the mother and tries to separate the son from the mother. This creates what Freud called castration anxiety in the son. This fear becomes the basis of what Freud called the super-ego, so the father is internalized as a threatening image, indeed as an enemy of the son's success in life.

It is true that if a newly married husband and wife have had a close bond with each other, the introduction of a child can create a great change. The father no longer has exclusive and unlimited physical access to his wife because a baby gets priority. A mother's powerful attachment to her children may, at least for a time, outweigh her feelings of closeness to her husband. Feeling that, the father may pull away and distance himself, or he may become very competitive with the children. He can become intolerant, anxious, possessive, refusing to share the mother's love. And he refuses to initiate his son into manhood.

The son faced with an Oedipal father has a father who is an enemy rather than an initiation-master.

The Oedipal father tends to be extremely repressive. He puts his sons into situations where they cannot grow. In family businesses, one sees children held under the father's thumb. He will not relinquish his power position and limits his children to positions of subservience. This type is graphically depicted in early Greek myth. The Sky God, Uranus, reacts with fear to a prediction that his son, Cronus, will grow up to overthrow him, so at the son's birth to the Earth Mother, Gaia, he attempts to forestall this by shoving the son back into the earth, symbolically back into the womb, and keeping him there. The father cannot endure the thought of being surpassed by his son and fears reprisal by the son. In the myth, this does indeed come to pass when Cronus eventually breaks out of bondage and succeeds in castrating his father. This pattern later repeats itself when Cronus is castrated by his repressed son, Zeus.

A son with an Oedipal father will develop a negative father complex and later project it on to men in authority over him. He will very likely be rebellious against them and try to overthrow them.

This kind of father is, in Jungian terms, a senex father, distant, cold and repressive.

The Too-Good Father. This is a father who is one-sidedly positive and does not allow his shadow side to show. He does not betray his son in any way but always accommodates and protects him. This has the effect of keeping the son at home and dependent on him. The message is: "I have this great, wonderful house and you will never do as well outside." The effective communication is: "You can't make it on your own, you aren't good enough, so you had better stay here with me. You need my protection, and I'm glad to provide it." The father offers comfort and security, but it is undermining because it prevents the son from testing himself in the real world and establishing his own sense of worth. This set-up is often seen in privileged classes. For sons who are heirs to fathers of great position or fortune, it is very difficult to achieve a true initiation and be released from "the father's house." If the father's house is too rich and accommodating and if the father is too good, if betrayal never happens, the son becomes father-bound.

The Third Circle: Anima

The Age of the Hero

We move next to the third circle in a man's evolving psychological development. It is the stage of the hero and presents another major challenge with which he must come to terms: the anima.

What is the anima? If the mother and father complexes constitute two basic structural strands in a man's personality, the anima can be thought of as a dynamic, transformative force. The anima constellates a man's creative energy and initiates the hero's journey in his development. The anima is generally imaged as feminine and conceptualized as the contrasexual feature of a man's masculine gender identity. She is his inner other, his soul mate.

It is important to note the essential difference between the anima and the mother complex. Both are feminine in nature, but the anima plays a very different role from the mother in a man's life. Whereas the mother stabilizes and contains his personality, the anima is dynamic and motivates him to find his own unique direction in life. The anima is the archetype of life itself, the life force. The Latin word *anima* means soul. She animates the psychic body as a force of vitality. She demands liveliness and change and ever further development, and she provides the energy and drive for the transformation that a man must go

43

through in order to pivot his identity from the father world to becoming his own man, free and independent. And, as all men know who have experienced her, she is not rational.

The anima demands that a man make an unqualified commitment to himself and to his own life. This is a challenge to responsibility. Men understandably have difficulty in taking this step because it means leaving the security of the world of father and mother. Out of fear, they become conservative and hold themselves back, keeping "a foot on the brake." They may have a problem with making the sacrifices demanded by the anima. They have reservations and doubts, fearing for a lack of inner resources to accomplish the task she sets before them. It seems impossible, not physically but psychologically and spiritually. It is brushed off as a silly dream, an illusion. They become frozen in established habits of mind. They renounce the heroic and settle for the conventional.

In myth, fairy tale and imaginative literature, the anima's challenge is classically depicted as the task of winning the hand of the beautiful young woman or freeing her from captivity. Marrying her symbolizes a man's achievement of making a lasting connection to the soul and committing himself to her "till death do us part."

While the process of confronting, winning, and integrating the anima belongs classically to midlife, a man will meet up with the anima throughout life in different forms, usually in discovering a remarkable woman with suitable features and attributes and projecting his anima onto her. This can begin early in life. A little boy can fall in love with a playmate or an older woman who is not his mother, such as a nurse, a teacher, or a cousin. In adolescence, the anima may appear when a boy falls in love with a movie star or a beautiful unattainable woman. In all cases, he will experience the archetypal passions of romantic longing, jealousy, and helpless infatuation. Eventually, he may meet the anima in a more accessible form and persuade her to marry him. One of the purposes of the anima is to draw a man out of his familiar parental context and into an unfamiliar interpersonal and cultural world. She stimulates "exogamous libido"— non-incestuous Eros—so that he leaves mother and father behind and ventures out into the wider world. The classical, full-blown "anima call" occurs at midlife, after a man has established himself in the father world and has made all the necessary investments in his life as a member of collective society.

There are many literary examples of the irrational power of the anima in a man's life. One of my favorites is Shakespeare's Cleopatra. At her beckoning, Mark Antony abandons his role as a dutiful member of the ruling triumvirate in Rome and lives with the exotic Cleopatra in her home in Egypt. Eventually he loses his life for her sake, and she for his. It is a cautionary tale about the dangers of anima possession. One of Jung's favorite literary anima figures was the larger than life feminine character in H. Rider Haggard's 19th century novel, *She*. Also set in Egypt, this story takes place in the dark interior of the country where a man discovers an immortal feminine figure known as "She Who Must Be Obeyed." Her power is overwhelming and utterly irresistible. Moreover, she is ancient and privy to the secrets of death and rebirth: she can go up in flames like a phoenix and transform herself into a youthful maiden. When she calls, a man finds her irresistible. For Jung, this figure illustrated the power of the anima in setting the course of a man's life. He himself alludes to such an experience in his famous Red Book.

When a man meets the anima in life, he feels an overwhelming desire to get close to her. She represents a promise of transformation and fulfillment. In her presence, a man discovers himself as if for the first time. He is a new man. The anima promises transformation, physical and spiritual. If he can only unite his life with hers, he feels, she will make him a new man and even immortalize him. However, he will also feel danger in her vicinity—she can destroy him.

The anima is an ambiguous figure—attractively wild and destructive and at the same time rejuvenating and creative. When she makes her appearance at midlife, she ignites a meltdown of fixed structures and identifications. She claims a man as her own and draws him into the fire of her transformative energy.

As a muse she inspires poetry and big dreams. A goddess, she elicits absolute devotion. The troubadour movement of the Middle Ages was an anima manifestation on a collective level, and she is the Beloved of the Romantic Tradition. She is represented in mythologies throughout the world—as Aphrodite, Freya, and Parvati, to name only a few.

The devastation that ensues when she is rejected or lost is dramatic. In Richard Wagner's "Ring," the first work, "Das Rheingold," tells of Wotan's promise to give Freia, the Love Goddess, to the grotesque Giants, Fafnir and Fasolt, in payment for the construction of his grandiose palace, Valhalla. Among the gods, the loss of Freya creates a crisis because it means they will gradually age, lose their beauty and die. A single day without her sees the apples in her orchard wither and rot and the gods becoming old, ill and decrepit. The rest of the drama follows from the gods' urgent quest to retrieve her and to bring back her powers of rejuvenation. She is the anima of the gods, and as such she is the source of life, of *joie de vivre* and *élan vital*.

It is in relation to the anima that a man experiences his profoundest sense of play and creativity, as well as his most complete freedom and sense of release from mundane cares. If an anima-endowed woman accepts a man into relationship with her, it is as if he is allowed reentry into paradise. She is the source of joy, of life itself and all its pleasures.

Anima versus Persona

It can be safely assumed that the anima will be the enemy of the persona. Persona defines a man's social identity as it is formed in conformity with others' expectations and rooted in his acceptance of roles and positions as offered by the father world. Persona takes shape through a gradual process of imitation, education, adaptation, and identification. It is based on mirroring what is seen in the immediate social environment or alternatively reacting against the surrounding milieu. It is not a superficial aspect of the personality. It originates in early childhood. In order to relate first to his mother and father, a son becomes a certain kind of little person and begins to develop a social identity, positive or negative, within the family context. Among peers, he eventually finds a niche as a particular kind of boy—the smart one, the handsome one, the athletic one, the popular one, the bad one, and so on. These are all personas, and they constitute the interface between a man and the social world surrounding him. They signal the world as to what roles this man may be expected to fill.

While parents are the earliest and most important contributors to this social identity, peers are later very important as well. Erik Erikson's definition of "psychosocial identity" offers an apt account of the persona: it is an agreement between oneself and important others regarding who and what kind of person one is. In adolescence, as Erikson famously wrote, the persona becomes an acute issue as the adolescent focuses intensely on what his peers think of him. The persona question is: "How do I relate to the group, and how do others in the group see me?" Loss of face amounts to disgrace and can lead to severe emotional consequences.

At its best, the persona gives a man the security of knowing that he has a place in the world. It provides a basis for his social standing in the community. From this position, he can exert power and influence. In addition, it provides a tool with which he can try to master his inner life. Through identification with his persona, anything in his inner life that does not seem to fit his picture of himself can be pushed aside. He is thus able to channel his energies into his work and build up a material position in the world.

The anima's entrance on the scene creates tremendous tension and instability as she challenges a man's commitment to the persona and opens a breach in his defenses against troublesome yearnings for deeper emotional satisfaction. She can motivate a man to leave mother and father, wife and family, and all official duties in order to abandon himself to the sheer joy of life in a moment of exuberance and passionate excess. In the world of opera—think of La Traviata—the anima typically rules. A typical operatic conflict involves a man torn between his duty to father, king, mother, or wife and his love for an unconventional woman. Such a conflict in life arises from the difference between the intentions of anima and the conventional demands of persona.

When the persona is firmly in place and the ego has strongly accepted and identified with it, the anima classically comes in to compensate—to blast away, to say it more dramatically, the identification with the persona. The purpose of this is to initiate a man's individuation. The classic story of individuation begins at midlife when the persona clashes with a will demanding that the man become more than his persona—unique, special, and different from the collective average. The source of this demand is the anima, thus she always appears as unconventional.

The appearance of the anima typically induces the "meltdown" of a man's persona structures and identifications. She calls for fluidity and flexibility, which contradict a man's entrenched notions and habits. Those fixities become the targets of her aggression, and the more deeply embedded they are the more she will attack them. She is then at her most dangerous, but the potential is also present for her greatest creative contribution to the possibilities for transformation and individuation. A collateral danger is that a man becomes anima possessed and loses all common sense and rationality. This is a kind of madness. On the other hand, the individuation potential lies in undergoing a transformation that forever frees a man from his previous dependencies and from identification with his persona. By bringing him out of this bondage to the past, she will lead him ultimately to the self. As the father was a bridge out of the mother into the outer world where the son established his persona, the anima is the bridge inward to the self. This is the meaning of her implacable opposition to the persona.

The uninitiated man will relate to the anima primarily with fear. She is too much for him because he has not integrated enough of the father's gift of masculinity. He is not able to claim an anima figure in real life even if he will dream of one in his fantasies. Initiation into the masculine prepares a man for his encounter with the anima.

On the other end of the spectrum, the man who has been well initiated into the masculine world of the father and is exceptionally successful in his persona adaptation runs the risk of "selling his soul" for the sake of gaining power and social position. The anima lure is so demanding of major change in direction and attitude that he will not even remotely consider the possibility of transformation. He remains stuck in the father world and cannot individuate further.

The anima, it must be emphasized, is not a derivative from the mother complex or archetype. She is *sui generis*, a psychic being unto herself and having her own independent foundation in the self. Actually, the anima is opposed to the mother. Part of the anima's function is, in fact, to free a man decisively from the mother and all she represents. Nor is the anima derived from the father, although a father's anima has a powerful effect on his son. The father's anima has a role to play in the relationship with the son—she can bind the son to his father. But again, the role of a man's anima is to separate him from his father as she does from his mother. She is an individuating power and demands that he become his own man, free and clear.

One can mark a distinction between three different kinds of bondage in men: the mother-bound, the father-bound, and the anima-bound. A mother-bound man, as described earlier, is typically weak, non-assertive, soft, and restricted in his phallic activities both with women and at work. A father-bound man is typically identified with the patriarchy and its structures in the social world: He is conservative, rigid, dogmatic, and tied to the persona. He is the man who sits at the right hand of the father and stays there, slowly going grey and becoming withered. The anima-bound man is typically a romantic and a dreamer. He is moody, unrealistic, overly emotional and sensitive; he is a permanent adolescent. It can happen that a mature and fully initiated man becomes temporarily anima-possessed through falling in love with a young woman who carries his anima projection. When this happens, he loses his judgment and values; he daydreams and finds it difficult to pay full attention to the details of daily life. He becomes inflated, dreaming big and unrealistic dreams about a perfect future together with his anima woman. He may be inspired to write poetry or sing youthful songs; he uncharacteristically spends money freely and without thought. Powerful emotions of sexual passion and murderous jealousy assault him, and extremes of ecstatic joy and despair alternate in rapid succession. He is temporarily anima-possessed.

A mother-bound man cannot feel these excesses. He does not fall powerfully in love with an anima woman because the mother effectively blocks the anima. The mother sits in the doorway, guarding the threshold. The man is locked in the mother's house, and the anima cannot enter. A father-bound man will, on the other hand, fall into anima-possession, since the purpose is to free him from the father complex and its insistence on conventionality. If he is strongly tied to the father, seated at his right hand and identified with an adapted and well socialized persona, he will manage to resist the possession. He will remain true to the father's world of collective rules and social norms.

A man's individuation task at midlife is to use the anima experience differently from the way he did in adolescence. In adolescence and early adulthood, the function of the anima is to "trick a man" and take him away from the mother and into a relationship with a woman, into marriage and family life. At midlife, the anima's function is to loosen identification with the persona. A man then can open an inner space where depth psychological experience has a place to operate.

At this stage of life, the anima experience becomes the opportunity for further development of a man's personality. As long as a man is identified with the persona and with his social roles in the world, personality is nothing more than an inconvenient nuisance. It just gets in the way. It has no functional value and is regarded as "mere emotionality." Personality has no place in the world of business deals, legal transactions, or peace treaties. The anima is seen as an enemy in the father world of the bottom line.

How can a man reconcile the two? They form a pair of opposites that must be held in tension. Dealing with the anima experience at midlife calls for establishing and holding this tension between desire and reality. This is a classic conflict and a man has to wait it out and tolerate the pain. Eventually an option will open up that offers a decision that would be neither exclusively a persona nor an anima decision but a "third" possibility that alchemically combines the two or transcends them.

The anima typically introduces inflation in a man's sense of himself and makes him feel bigger than life. She creates an illusion that he is "God's gift," and he feels wonderful in her presence, powerful and healthy. In a sense, this is not altogether bad. It gives the courage and energy to undertake heroic tasks for her sake. The paradoxical nature of this condition demonstrates the problem with deciphering the messages of the anima: which are true and which are nonsense? A man does feel himself to be God's gift, yet he knows he is one of billions of such gifts; he can be a hero for her, but his capacities may be exaggerated beyond his possibilities. The experience of being unique and special and capable of heroics does put him in touch with something true and can be useful if picked up and used in the right way. Thus, in one way, the anima brings inflationary illusion, but in another she reveals truth as well.

The anima in her own nature is not realistic according to the standards understood by the persona and the man's ego awareness. She would turn the world into a chaotic place where each man would be a law unto himself. This is the philosophy of anarchists and dictators. A man who is possessed by the anima feels he can do as he pleases. Reality contradicts this approach to the world, however. Sooner or later he will run afoul of the rules of society and face the consequences. A man cannot tell a judge he was under the influence of something other than law or that he "forgot himself" and be let off the hook of impersonal justice.

Odysseus dealt very successfully with the anima in his encounter with Circe. In a manifestation of the negative transformative power of the anima, Circe turns men into swine. Such men, who have completely believed the anima mirage and given in to the enticement of pleasure fulfillment, can be said to have lost human consciousness; their ego has been demolished. With Hermes' advice, Odysseus is able to make a relationship with her, getting her to commit herself to his safety and the welfare of his men before he goes to bed with her. He and his crew are then able to remain on her island renewing themselves before continuing on their journey, thus gleaning the rejuvenating benefit of the anima experience without falling prey to her negative, destructive capabilities.

The anima is the unconscious, which needs to be brought into a human relationship. Jung often said that the unconscious does not know what the ego and the ego world are about and must be taught. One of the roles of the active imagination is to accomplish that instruction—to tell the unconscious what the needs and demands of real life are, because she does not know and must be convinced. One needs Odysseus' strategy of beginning with tough bargaining (he holds Circe at sword point, threatening her and extracting promises before bedding her) and then knowing when to give in. When done successfully, a man can contain the effects of the anima, neither falling into them or acting them out, nor repressing and ignoring them. He then develops the inner capacity to be inspired and creative. The anima becomes his own animation, and gradually personality comes into being. Learning to love his moods, his musings, and his creative, unconventional thoughts, he begins to learn the joy of giving in to irrational notions. It is very releasing to allow oneself to be irrational. A man can be a poet with life, becoming unpredictable and inconsistent. It is exhilarating and playful—the anima becomes a playmate as the man learns to play in his inner world.

Playing and intimacy are closely related. If one cannot play, one cannot become intimate. A man's attractiveness to a woman depends very much on his ability to be intimate. Through the anima, a man can learn to become intensely intimate. On his integration of the anima, a man can enhance his inner capacity to enter a playful mood and become childish without fear.

The anima, when she is developed in a part of a man's life as a companion or inner felt-presence, tempers his anger and disappointments in life. By the time a man is middle-aged, he has usually built up a great store of anger and disappointment about his life. Perhaps his children have not turned out as he would like; or his wife is no longer what she was. Maybe he himself is not what he was physically or mentally, or his career has not been what he had hoped. He may have become embittered and generally ill tempered. The presence of the anima counteracts all that, giving a kind of mellow feeling and soothing the anger. She allows for play and offers a sense of being able to start over.

She permits intimacy in momentary relationships, on a weekend or at a luncheon, without requiring the presence of a woman to enable becoming relational. Men characteristically have great difficulty becoming intimate and relational without having a woman to accomplish it for them. The formality of an all-male group, for example, can be radically changed with the advent of an anima woman. A man who has integrated the anima is able to achieve intimacy and relationality without reliance on a woman. He can make his own relationships, which can be *eros* relationships; he can become intimate with men and women and children and beasts because he has that inner capacity.

The anima also enables a man to be imaginative. As the spinner of images and fantasies, she helps him to let himself entertain illusions without necessarily believing in them. The ego and the anima forge a bond in a permanent relationship. A man then becomes a personality and consequently leaves the patriarchy, which is his identification with the father. As long as the anima/princess is attached to the king, a man cannot get out of the patriarchy and win his soul away from his persona attachments. On winning her away from her embeddedness in the patriarchy, the hero has his own soul. A man, then, has his personality, including his affectivity, his emotional life, and his interiority.

Failure to Win the Anima

At this point, it is useful to restate the observation that the embodied anima is an unconventional female. If the man is too much still in the mother, the anima, because she is physically female, will resonate too closely to the mother and threaten further regression into the mother. It is for this reason that a man still stuck in the mother cannot truly fall in love with an anima woman. Not only does the mother sit at the doorway and block the anima, but because the anima is physically female, she is too close to the mother. A man thus must resist the female or risk further regression into the mother. He will not, then, see a woman as attractive, because that would bring him too close to incest.

If a man is too much in the father, the unconventionality of the anima woman is what threatens him, not the fact that she is female. It is a more conscious threat, then. In the movie *Fatal Attraction*, we see a man drawn into a wild, destructive anima with disastrous consequences, which is how a man yet embedded in the father will perceive the dangers of the unconventional female. A man too much in the father can successfully fall in love, marry, and lead a conventional family life, but he cannot afford to experience the anima fully because she threatens his bond to the father. Behind this, clinging to embeddedness in the father and the patriarchy, is actually the threat of regression into the mother; for if the father bond is loosened, the bridge out of the mother disappears; and the son is drawn back into the mother. The consequences for such a man, lacking the inner resources from having integrated the father in order to leave the mother, may be massive regression or psychotic break. His commitment to the world of the father is based on a defense against the mother. The separation from the mother has not taken place enough for him to let go of the father. Because the anima's unconventionality seeks to free him from the father, she is a profound threat; and he will resist her.

To the mother-bound man, then, the anima is a threat because she is female. To him, she appears as a witch, an evil monster. To the father-bound man, the anima is a threat because she is unconventional. To him, she appears as a seductress and a deceiving siren.

Among mother-bound men, we can identify four positions along a spectrum from more to less mother-bound. First, we note the man without an anima. This is a man deeply embedded in the mother and not at all attracted to women, to the point that he simply does not see them. Typically, his father has been absent or unable to help his son out of the mother. Actually, he is the man described above in the chapter on the mother as the man without a mother. He is embedded in an archetypal mother. His real mother was not there enough for him to be drawn out into the object world. His anima is in the unconscious. She is "unconstellated," belonging to the *massa confusa* of undifferentiated material in the unconscious.

Somewhat less embedded in the mother is the man with the prematurely integrated anima. He tends to be effeminate. There is an identity mix because male and female were not strongly separated at the earlier stage of leaving the mother and identifying with the father. Masculine and feminine elements are mixed, so that the ego takes on a coloration that is slightly more feminine than normal. While it might seem that he has integrated the anima in his connection to the feminine, there is actually a lack of differentiation between the masculine and the feminine. He may be rather aesthetic, exhibiting certain feminine and maternal characteristics. He sees the mother in females. The female body remains identified with the mother's body: a woman's breasts are her breasts, and the vagina is horrifying and threatening rather than sweet and alluring.

Third, we come to the man with a lesbian anima. He is in love with women who prefer other women. He can be attracted to women and make love to them, but he does so as if he himself were a woman. His lover must also be a woman; *eros* is a woman-to-woman experience. Again, this is a result of remaining "in the mother."

Fourth is the man with the fleeting anima, the Don Juan. He seems to be a man's man, powerfully attracted to women, sexually active, and generally promiscuous. While he may exhibit behavior that suggests a love of women, there is actually no underlying love of a specific woman at all. There is sexuality without *eros*; there is no affection for them. The anima is still not constellated optimally. He is a heartless lover, who is actually still mother-bound and has not identified with the father. Differentiation between masculine and feminine has not yet taken place definitively.

Among men still in the father, I will describe two positions. The man with the perfectionistic anima is so tied by love of the father that the passion of the anima does not have a feminine form. He is fiercely committed to the father and the father's world. In the fierceness and the dedication to ideals and notions of perfection and spiritual purity, one senses the anima. The love involved, however, is not feminine but rather like the love as the Holy Spirit that passes between the Father and Son in the Trinity. Certain classical forms of Christianity have a powerful exponent of that type of commitment to the Father, such that the anima stays in the father world and within the father-son bond. This type of man may marry a woman in order to be close to a powerful man; the woman's father is the one he is really in love with.

A variation of the man with a perfectionistic anima is one who is himself perfectionistic, dedicated to high ideals and purity of a spiritual, ascetic, or aesthetic nature. Certain kinds of writers or artists fall into this category, exhibiting great refinement and perfection. One misses the anima messiness in their spiritual, precise, Olympian work. Another example is the enthusiastic priest who only loves God the Father, has dedicated heart and soul to the highest ideals of religion and philosophy, and who has seemingly transcended sexuality or transmuted it into religious enthusiasm.

At the other end of the spectrum of men stuck in the father is the man with a conventional anima. By definition, however, the anima is unconventional. In this case she has not appeared fully or authentically, having been unable to reveal her full presence because the man is trapped in the father. This man is married conventionally, his wife is conventional, his children are conventional, and his career is conventional. Everything is middle-of-the-road; he is dedicated to maintaining the status quo and enhancing the persona and patriarchal values. The anima's un-conventional presence in this man is occluded by the presence of the father; he is actually married to the father. This man is not interested in separating the anima from the father, since he is committed to staying married to the father.

When a man is sufficiently separated from the world of the mother through initiation into the world of the father, and when the male identity is secure and consolidated enough as an inner structure so that he can leave the father, he can then allow the anima to approach him nakedly and powerfully. He will not need to be defensive towards her. He will be able to pursue the task of winning her from the father; and once she is won, he will be able to marry her. The marriage of the hero to the anima means that a relatively stable and permanent relationship comes about between a man whose masculine identity is firm and the feminine. He is able to be in the world of the fathers, the persona world, and to be effective in it, but not be totally *of* it. He is able to be unconventional, to be playful, to let himself float about in fantasy and liminality. He can become intensely intimate without fear of losing himself because he has the necessary inner structures. He can be creative and think un-conventional thoughts; he can experiment and risk his feelings.

Once this relationship with the anima is established, they can have children. The child born of this relationship between the anima and the ego is a new self. Anima development means developing the personality through intimate contact with and knowledge of his emotional life. This is the era of integrating emotional life, of becoming a personality. The man with a developed relationship to the anima has a personality and is a personality. As a result of that, he is able to go on to encounter and experience the Self as a new being.

A brief aside

One of Jung's first discoveries occurred when he was a resident early in the 1900s and doing research with the Word Association Experiment (WAE). Using this instrument, he found that similarities in the organization of complexes could be identified in families. The responses of a mother and a daughter, for example, would indicate very similar complexes. This finding could be said to be the beginning of family systems theory. Although Jung never followed up on it in any major way, other researchers have found evidence for continuities of complexes through generations. They are called cultural complexes or in some cases generational complexes. A trauma to a family at one point in history, for example the suicide or homicide of a father, can perseverate through generations. The collective memory of the event and the impact on the wife and children can be passed on to two, three, four or more subsequent generations. This phenomenon has been extensively studied in countries within the former Soviet Union.

One of Jung's early studies concerned the role of the father in the destiny of the individual.[2] Jung discussed the influence of the father complex on children, both daughters and sons. His discussion was based on the finding that family systems rest upon

---

[2] C.G. Jung, 1909. "The Significance of the Father in the Destiny of the Individual," *CW* 4, pars. 693-744.

complex structures and that these complexes are passed on from parents to children. This transmission of unconscious complex arrangements down through the generations is well described in the colloquial expression, "the apple doesn't fall far from the tree."

The way a father relates to his own anima and his level of anima development will thus have an impact on his son and the way the anima will constellate in the son. This is not biologically genetic but is passed on through psychic influence and transmission, through subtle behavioral gestures and modeling. In identifying with the father, the son introjects not only the persona of the father but aspects of his unconscious as well. The father's internal dynamics—the relation between his ego and his anima, and the way he has dealt with "the anima problem" in his own life—will have an impact on the son's approach to the same inner figure.

Optimally, the father will have dealt with the anima effectively, integrated it, and become a personality, so that his relationship to the anima had become one of free exchange between consciousness and unconsciousness. If the father's *eros* is free and not bound in the father or mother structures, the son will experience this. The son may witness this in seeing the father not being bound to the wife (he is not "henpecked"), which would indicate a mother-bound anima. Or, the son might witness father-boundedness in seeing his father as conventional or perfectionistic.

Optimally, a son would see in his father a free and integrated anima development, and he could witness in his father a freedom to love and work, unbound by either matriarchy or patriarchy. If a son sees a free father, his chances of being able to free his anima later in and for life will be that much greater.

A number of problems, as we have suggested, can appear. If, for example, the father's anima is attached to the patriarchy, the father will be conventional and perfectionistic. The son might then have a tendency to rebel against that or else to follow in his father's footsteps by imitating him. It can also happen that the father's anima compensates for a cold mother. She may have been an emotionally cold woman married to her opposite—as often happens—that is, to a warm and extraverted type of husband. The father becomes very close to the son at an early age, while the mother remains more or less distant in the background. A maternal father compensates possibly with too much intimacy and *eros* toward the son, which will create later problems. The son will become too emotionally bound to the father and search for father figures who play a similar role rather than functioning as mentors to guide him further into the world, thus retarding development of his independence.

Problems will also arise if the father's anima is locked up in the mother. The father might be the Don Giovanni type, for example, in which case his anima image is free from his mother, but not its affect. In other words, he can pursue women and have sexual relations with them, but the feeling of being in love is blocked. Underneath his promiscuous behavior, he is mother bound; his *eros* is still truly attached to the mother. If the son sees his father is of this type, philandering while his wife becomes hurt and embittered, the son usually is unable to identify with his father. He takes the side of his mother against the father in what becomes a family struggle. Because he sees his father's anima projections rampant in the world, his own sexuality becomes inhibited. He tends to become a "good boy," defender of his mother and mother-rights, and overly faithful to mother figures and women's prerogatives over a man's freedom of *eros* and movement. His own sexuality tends to be blocked. He is likely to take care of mother or mother figures against father, even marrying a woman in order to take care of her. With the father being himself so mother-bound, development of his son's in-dependence and freedom is, again, retarded.

In the circle of the anima, typically, a man experiences this psychic figure through projection, often onto an unconventional woman with whom he falls in love. As his anima, she represents his future psychological development into the so-called classic phases of individuation. He has the problem, however, of how to relate to this figure who is carrying the soul for him in projection. The question is whether to go off with her, marry her, and have children with her, or to treat the experience symbolically as an inner challenge, as the onset of a search that will take him to the inner depths of the psyche rather than to an outer relationship, which may end up only repeat prior relationships. How may he solve this anima problem in such a way as to create the optimal individuation step? This question arises in addition to and complicating further the obvious ethical and moral questions attendant to the situation.

When a purely inner solution is sought, the man takes the experience as a constellation or projection of the anima and uses classical Jungian methods for working with it (such as active imagination, dream analysis, and so on), avoiding any action on the interpersonal level with the "outer person," so to speak. This strategy usually results in sterility; there is no "child" of the relationship. It becomes virtually autoerotic. Outer manifestations of this outcome are often states of depression, lack of animation, rage, a kind of unfulfilled, woundedness or sense of deprivation.

Reflections of this condition are played out in myth. In Greek myth, Zeus the Father falls in love with and impregnates Semele. She asks to see Zeus, whom she has only seen at night because of the dangers of seeing him as he really is. He is finally persuaded to reveal himself to her; but the heat and brilliance of his appearance burns Semele to a cinder. Zeus snatches their fetus from her body and implants it in his thigh where it matures. The resultant child is Dionysus, the god of ecstasy, intoxication, wine—a woman's god. When Hera learns of all this, she is enraged by Zeus's infidelity and, more, his usurpation of the woman's prerogative of giving birth. She elects to pursue the course of parthenogenesis herself, which she accomplishes three times, bearing Hephaistos, Ares, and Typhon. Hephaistos is born crippled with feet turned back, suffering low self-esteem and ridicule. He represents woundedness, reflecting the lameness that can be the result of the parthenogenesis inherent in trying to solve the anima problem purely internally. The second son, Ares, becomes the God of War; he is the aggression and rage that can follow such a solution. Typhon, the third son, exemplifies an even more extreme rage reaction: typhoons—tremendous upheavals in nature—are associated with this god, suggesting violence and severe emotional instability as consequences of this inner solution.

These offspring, then, represent the emotional aftereffects of an aborted anima integration relegated entirely to the inner level; they are not positive, "natural" children of the resolution and offer no future for the psyche. Jung spoke of "regressive restoration of the persona," wherein a man deeply enmeshed in an anima crisis—instead of going through the entire experience and coming out on the other side more integrated—regresses and tries to restore the persona, resuming his prior identity and trying to "tough it out." Characteristically, such men do become depressed, wounded, angry, and unfulfilled.

If a purely outer solution to the anima problem is sought, a man may get a divorce, marry again and possibly begin a second family. If his actions are the result of a purely outward solution, based on impulse and instinct lacking any reflection on what he is doing, they will be repeated again and again. The relation-ships will develop along very similar lines; the reasons a relationship does not work out with one woman will be the same reasons one will not work out with the next.

What kind of solution, then, should be pursued? What is the answer? Occasionally, one or the other of these two solutions turns out to be the best in a specific situation. Certainly, the outcome should reflect that a relationship has been established; there should be, indeed, a marriage in the sense of a permanent bond between the ego and the anima. In the Brothers Grimm fairytale, "The White Snake," as in many other European fairytales, the hero does successfully court and marry the anima figure, thus symbolizing a bond between a man's ego conscious-ness and the anima unconscious.

The child born of this union between the ego and the anima symbolizes the Self. To this offspring we can apply the term *spiritus rector*—guiding spirit. This child will guide the ego in its further quest for meaning and purpose. The resolution of the confrontation between the anima and the ego must include somehow, at some level, a marriage—a sense of a permanent bond between ego and anima—be it predominantly inner or predominantly outer, or both. An exclusively inner or exclusively outer solution falls short; there must be some kind of combination. There has to be an outer relationship or the resolution will be autoerotic; there must be an inner sense of meaning of the relationship, otherwise it is purely repetitious.

Finally, there must be an outcome of this relationship beyond itself. The relationship with the anima is not an end in itself, even though our fairy tale does end at this point. The *spiritus rector* ("guiding spirit") is truly a love child evolving through the experience between a man's conscious ego and personality and the anima representing his irrational, wild, unconventional, feminine side. This union takes place outside the bounds established by father and mother. The love child is always born outside the bounds of matrimony. It represents a certain freedom from law and convention; the child will also be unconventional.

Obviously a fine line exists between the love child and the problem bastard child. The love child is the successful outcome of the confrontation with the anima only if it is symbolic and not concrete or literal. If he is concrete, he is literally a bastard, born outside wedlock. He will constitute a problem by representing acting out and will be an outcast in the father world, always rebellious, envious, seeking to overthrow the world of order and structure. In order to be a successful outcome, the love child must then be a symbolic child, the fruit of the union appearing in non-biologic form. But even if he is concretized in any other way, for example as a book, artwork, or project, the consequence will be the repetitiousness discussed above; because, when the product is completed, it is finished, and there is no enduring value to the psyche. If the child is held at the symbolic level, it is not lost to the psyche but can direct from within. It is maintained at the level of psyche reality, rather than embodied and lost at the level of literal reality. Optimally, then, the product of the union is the symbolic child, the *spiritus rector*.

An example of this symbolic child is Hermes. Hermes is the product of the love union between Zeus (married to Hera, representing the law of marriage) and the nymph Maia. As the offspring of the patriarchal dominant, Zeus, and the unconventional other woman, Maia, Hermes will become a crucial figure in Greek mythology and later in alchemy. Born in a cave, Hermes does extraordinary deeds on the first day of his life. He creatively invents the lyre out of a turtle's shell and then, hungry, goes to Apollo's herds to steal some cattle (he is god of thieves). Mightily angry, Apollo takes Hermes before Zeus the judge. Zeus reconciles the brothers, and there is an exchange of gifts—the lyre for the cattle. Apollo becomes, then, the god of music as Hermes becomes the god of shepherds. Through this relationship between Hermes and Apollo, the Greeks found a balance between a spirit of rationality represented by Apollo and the liminality of Hermes, the god of irrationality, thieves, night, sudden inspirations, shamans. Where Apollo operates on rationality, Hermes operates on chance.

By reconciling these two children of Zeus, the Greeks sought a balance between these two attitudes toward life, both of which are necessary to a man's wholeness. Without Apollo's rationality, a man has little stability; but without Hermes' spirit, a man lacks inventiveness and inspiration. Had Hermes not been accepted into the pantheon, the irrationalist outsiders might have engendered a revolutionary overthrow of the "regulars." Thus the inclusion of Hermes in the pantheon is an attempt by the Greek spirit to reach an inclusive, pluralistic, and democratic solution to spiritual variation in the population. In Christian tradition, the same accommodation is achieved in the variations among the saints.

Eventually Hermes becomes the guide, a messenger god carrying Zeus's messages to mortals. Psychologically speaking, he represents intuition. If one is well connected with Hermes, one knows what the Self wants and can consult the Self on the complex decisions of life. Hermes personifies, then, the *spiritus rector*—the consultative guiding spirit between the ego and the Self. The messages from the Self can take the form of dreams (Hermes is the god of dreams), synchronicities (chance events), or doors opening—which are often how life's problems are solved. Hermes sets the process in motion.

In the Bible we find the instructive story of David and Bathsheba, the voluptuous wife of David's leading military general Uriah. David sees Bathsheba in all her naked glory while bathing on her rooftop terrace, and decides he must have her for himself, so he arranges to have Uriah killed in battle and takes Bathsheba as his wife. Their union turns out to be quite satisfactory, and one of their children is the successor king to David, the wise Solomon. One could read this as the birth of the symbolic spiritus rector. David develops into a famous poet and writer, largely one would assume as a result of his anima connection, and he dies peacefully, old and rich.

The Fourth Circle: Self

The Age of the Mature Man

In the fourth circle, we move from the age of the hero to the age of the mature man, and here the Self presents the central challenge. At this point, we are considering a man who has reached the fourth circle of personality development, which is quite advanced. Most men in everyday walks of life have not come this far. Commonly, they are caught still in some way in the circles of the mother or the father or remain fixed in the hero identity. If they register the psyche at all, it is in an unconscious and projected form, perhaps in the movies or on television where the psychic world is acted out before their eyes. They have relatively little self-awareness or consciousness of an inner world and its features. They do not pay attention to their dreams and spend no time in trying to understand their meaning for their own lives. They are living in two dimensions, not in the third as offered by contact with the unconscious.

We are now speaking about the second half of life and the movement toward the fifth circle, which is concerned with life's ultimate transcendent meaning. Men who have entered into these late stages of individuation have had a good deal of life experience and have achieved considerable self-awareness and consciousness. Often, they are highly successful professionally and socially. They have also arrived at a sense of inner reality and an awareness of the complexes—the attractive pull of the mother, the father, the anima, and so on—and they have separated and come to terms with them. Such a man is in command of himself but also aware that he is not in charge of his destiny. The ego has entered into a subservient relationship to the greater personality, the Self.

Out of the confrontation and interaction with the anima that takes place in the third circle, a *spiritus rector* is born in the fourth. The presence of this psychic function has several typical features. A man who is connected with an inner guide no longer takes his most important cues from the collective or the consensus of the group (persona considerations), either with regard to his individual life choices or his public positions. He is Self-directed, oriented from within by a personal vision for himself and by ever emerging greater self-knowledge. He has his own myth. His vision for life is not necessarily based on a dramatic "road to Damascus" experience. It could be less explicit and function as an intuitive sense of self that orients him. The guidance function may be partially unconscious to him. It operates like an internal gyroscope.

The *spiritus rector* is an uncanny guide. This is because it does not appear to be rational by usual standards. Its directives and messages imply a large unconscious plan or vision for life, a pre-set course of a life process that is not culturally determined and therefore not predictable. By making choices on the basis of strong intuitions and a felt sense of Self, an unconscious life plan emerges and is revealed over time. Socrates referred to this as the voice of his *daimon,* which he would consult when he had to make crucial decisions in his life, as when the Athenian court gave him the choice of drinking the cup of poisonous hemlock or going into exile. The *daimon* would only respond in the negative, otherwise it would remain silent. When Socrates asked if he should accept the hemlock, the *daimon* was silent. So he drank it without question or hesitation. Choices made on this basis are not rational in the usual sense, and Socrates had a difficult time defending his decision because it appeared to be suicide. His choice, however, followed his life plan: had he left Athens and gone into exile, he would not have been true to the fundamental essence of who Socrates was. He would not have been Socrates.

The *spiritus rector* gives one the felt sense of "this is me" or "this is not me." Writers will often say that it took years to find their "voice." Though they may have developed technical skill in school, they acknowledge that it is a different matter to discover their own signature style. That style, their "voice," involves a distinctive way of putting things, a rhythm and pattern of verbal expression that sounds true to them. The styles of Hemingway and Faulkner, for instance, are very different. This was not consciously worked out by their respective egos. Hemingway did not start out as an author by consciously deciding to write short sentences; he found that he was simply being Hemingway by writing that way—the taciturn macho male, the heroic fighter, and so on. A writer's style will be consistent with other things about his character, and it will represent his essence. This unique signature is the gift of the *spiritus rector*.

The manifestation of the *spiritus rector* is not restricted to intellectuals and accomplished artists. Everyone is capable of being an artist-in-life. As a man makes key choices in the second half of life, these begin to sketch in his essential features as a mature man. They are no longer mimics of his father's or his mother's styles. At midlife he begins to transcend those early influences.

Problems arise if a man lives his life without the integrity conferred by the *spiritus rector*. It is possible to deny or override its direction. A man can live instead by a conventional code of behavior, orienting himself according to the demands of the persona instead of the inner voice of the Self. One quickly notices in such men of a lack of courage to be authentic. In fact, these men are plentiful in all cultures. Such men may have lived socially successful and culturally circumspect lives, but they are not individuated men and they leave no unique impression when you meet them. They are company men, cut-outs of stereotypical patterns. The unique images that remain of such men as Carl Jung and Sigmund Freud, for example, are based on their essence. They each evolved a unique style by following the uncanny guidance of a *spiritus rector*. This factor pervades all levels of activity right down to the most concrete decisions of daily life. They are originals, not imitators.

This guidance is not rational, but that does not mean it is crazy or absurd. It means that the decisive choices in life cannot be simply derived from ante- cedents. If one knew everything possible about a man's genetic make-up and cultural and psycho-social history, one still could not predict what the *spiritus rector* would guide him to do next. If one knows enough about a person's background, his general character may be somewhat predictable from early on, but the details of his individuation process cannot be forecast. The mysterious essence of a man's personality is unknowable until it is made manifest in life. This sense of who one is, deeply, becomes more conscious to a man in the second half of life, after he has left his mother's lap and his father's home, has met the anima and discovered his personality, and has gone on to develop a sense of his own voice through tuning in to the *spiritus rector*.

As the essence of the Self becomes more consciously available to a man, its position moves from the unconscious toward the conscious side of the psyche. It's like the rising of the sun—distant but obviously manifest. The birth of the Self in con- sciousness is the result of the relationship established to the anima earlier, which has opened the door to the unconscious so that the *spiritus rector* can become a conscious function. The anima now becomes a psychological function as mediator and is no longer anthropomorphized or imaged as a feminine figure, but rather operates as a communication link with the Self. The anima, as such, has given way to the *spiritus rector*. She has opened the way to the Self and created a realm of inner space. This results in a new childlike ability to play spontaneously and be creative in an adult fashion. Think of Goethe in his later years.

Sometimes a vocational call for the remainder of a man's life will come about as the result of a strong encounter with the unconscious, that is, in a vision, a big dream or an impressive active imagination. I describe this kind of experience in the book, *In MidLife*. When Odysseus descends to the underworld to meet with Tiresias and ask for advice about how to return home to his beloved Ithaca, the blind seer tells him how to get home but says he cannot remain there permanently until he has completed another task. He instructs him to take an oar and travel so far inland that he finds people who do not know what oars are, and there he is to plant the oar in the earth. In short, Odysseus is asked to become a missionary of Poseidon, the god of the sea, whom Odysseus had offended by killing his son, the Cyclops Polyphemus, and who had therefore persecuted Odysseus by driving him hither and yon across the high seas without a chance of making his way home. He must take up this mission in order to expiate the wrathful god.

In other words, after one has gone through midlife a man does not find a permanent resting place or comfortable home. Instead, there is an imperative to do something more and not primarily for oneself. The imperative is one of service and has the aura of serving a purpose something beyond simple individual self-actualization. It means service to a deity, that is, becoming an agent of the Self.

After his midlife crisis, Jung said that he knew that he no longer belonged to himself alone but that he now belonged to the generality. He felt the need to share his experience and to speak about it in order to lead the consciousness of others further. He spent the rest of his life writing his books on psychology based on his midlife experience as recounted in *The Red Book*, named by him *Liber Novus*, his "New Testament." It became his mission in life to explicate the reality of the psyche. St. Paul's conversion and its consequences for his life can be seen similarly. In the moment when he was blinded by a bright light on the road to Damascus, he experienced a dramatic call from the Self that sustained him and gave his life meaning for the rest of his days. He poured his energy into his mission and became the Paul that we know from his later letters. He found his personal myth by understanding and incarnating the meaning of this numinous experience.

An important ethical question poses itself at this point in our reflections: How is a man to tell the difference between what I would call "a true mission" and a misguided mission that would be an enactment of pride, wounded self-esteem, early trauma, and resentment? The latter is also irrationally driven by unconscious complexes and may assume the trappings of a divine imperative. As was the case with Hitler, an "inner voice" can counsel evil. One can fall into the hands of evil and be as controlled by it as by good, and have the felt sense of being guided by a *spiritus rector*. It is a question of who or what one serves. Hitler will stand out forever as a man who was possessed by the spirit of evil. Sometimes the only thing that helps a man distinguish between the light and the dark is offered by a tradition of morals and ethics.

The vision brought by the *spiritus rector* in the form of a more conscious sense of the life plan helps a man organize his energy for the future. It provides a general orientation, though not usually specifics. It offers a symbol, and symbols suggest possible channels for the flow of psychic energy. A man without a guiding vision or personal myth does not know where to put his energy and so is dependent on others or on culture to give him direction. The emerging consciousness of the larger Self, given through the agency of the *spiritus rector,* is essential for channeling energy in an individual way in the second half of life because it suggests where meaningful activity is possible. Because the *spiritus rector* is a living presence in the psyche, it constitutes a continuous source of direction and inspiration. A man can go back to it in inner dialogue and be renewed in its vision. The symbol is supported by the anima, the life force, so it is invested with vitality.

A man's ground plan will become evident to him if he listens to the *spiritus rector* and pursues its direction honestly. Honesty is authenticity. One could say this is living authentically, as the existentialists put it, or religiously as Jung would express it.

The great Danish philosopher and theologian, Søren Kierkegaard, arranged the stages of personal development in three phases: the aesthetic, the ethical, and the religious. The first stage is based on the pleasure principle and seen in typical form in Mozart's opera, *Don Giovanni*. A man in this stage is locked in the mother circle of psychological development. He is a *puer aeternus*. The second stage introduces a sense of ethical values. Here, a man guides his life by the law and a corresponding sense of right and wrong, and he develops the ability to make difficult moral decisions in a lawyer-like manner. He is in the father circle and committed to the rule of law and living an ethical life. This stage is succeeded, or transcended, by the religious stage by means of what Kierkegaard calls a "leap of faith." This man is a hero, a "knight of faith." He manifests at a time in life when laws are inadequate or irrelevant to his challenges. The voice of the *spiritus rector* dominates in this stage, and it calls for obedience. The voice of the Self is not derived from the law but is rooted in the archetypal depths of the psyche. A man's sense of meaning is now contingent not upon pleasure or the satisfaction of instinctual desires, nor upon obedience to the law, but upon primary consideration of fulfilling the will of the Self. A vision grips a man and leads him beyond the limits of the law. Kierkegaard's biblical example is Abraham, who hears God's voice commanding him to sacrifice his son, Isaac, which countermands the law of fatherhood. He has left the circle of the father archetype and has entered the circle of the Self. It is a radical step into obedience to the Lawgiver and not to the law.

While there are many mundane instances of the guidance the *spiritus rector* provides in daily life, this step into the religious follows the *spiritus rector* into another realm of being, the spiritual. The moment when the ethical imperative is transcended by the spiritual imperative is ambiguous from the point of view of the law. It cannot be evaluated, justified, or defended by rules or law; it is its own imperative.

Earlier stages are not necessarily left behind in these later circles. They can be relativized in some important ways, but a man does not leave his shadow behind, that is his human flaws and weaknesses, his unsolved problems with mother, father, and anima. Earlier circles may now not be so bright but they are not ever completely deleted. There is always a residue of unresolved material in every life, even in that of a great person.

The Fifth Circle: God

The Age of the Sage

Moving into the discussion of the fifth circle, I will explore a stage of development that few men reach consciously, although everyone who lives into old age enters into it in one way or another, because it poses the question of the meaning of a man's life. We can see this stage expressed graphically in the biographies of famous men, such as the Russian novelist Leo Tolstoy and the philosopher Ludwig Wittgenstein. Both men in their own way took up the question of life's meaning and the question of God. Whether a man looks to established religious traditions or ventures into this search individually, the purpose is the same: to come into contact with the Ultimate, with the Ground of Being to use the phrase of Paul Tillich, and to search for the answer to the question of life's meaning.

As we shall see, this late phase of the individuation process involves deep engagement and struggle with the transcendent Self. This is not a simple matter of learning to meditate and to clear the mind of distracting thoughts. In truth, it means confronting the deepest paradoxes within oneself and within the cosmos, which are two aspects of a single reality. In this engagement one finds light and dark, the sources of life and death, and the energies of creation and destruction. One can think of it as a dialogue with the God within and beyond the limits of the psyche. In speaking of dialogue, I follow the Jewish thinker Martin Buber's writing on this subject and also Jung's account of his engagement with the biblical God image in his late work, *Answer to Job*. It is a serious engagement, an *Auseinandersetzung*.

It is because one connects to the *spiritus rector* in the fourth circle that one comes upon the problems of opposites in God and the Self. If one fails to achieve this connection in the fourth circle, one simply accepts conventional views and these more fundamental problems never arise. The experience of the *spiritus rector*, however, leads one to an encounter with the mixture within the Self of good and evil, masculine and feminine, and other polarities and paradoxes.

The advance of a man's age into the 7th and 8th decades typically brings an increasingly urgent need to gain a more complete perspective on the meaning and patterns in one's life, to develop a picture of the whole. Dark, brooding questions about what it all means and what it all amounts to are typical of people of advanced years at a certain stage in their reflections. They may be diagnosed with depression, but it is not that simple. This mood is not without meaning, and it is not fundamentally biological in origin. It is existential. As they review their lives, these men often dwell on certain key decisions and turning points in their personal history, for good or ill, in attempts to come to terms with the choices they have made in life. Often this is presented as a moral issue: Did I do the right thing? Or it may be more of an emotional question like: Did I follow my passion enough or did I avoid its call? This reflection in old age is an attempt to find answers to the question of meaning in the specific life that has been lived and to come to a just and balanced appreciation of it. The soul is placed on a scale and its weight measured against a feather, as the ancient Egyptians thought of judgment in the afterlife. This can be a long and drawn out reflection. The alchemists called it *meditatio*, the long meditation involving inner dialogues with good and bad angels, and it begins with *nigredo*, the realm of the raven in alchemical imagery.

Beyond simply reflecting on their personal lives, men in old age turn philosophical and consider the meaning of human life itself. Why do human beings exist at all? Is our presence on this planet, our beautiful and awesome Earth, a good thing or a bad thing? What is the meaning of human consciousness in the vast universe of stars and galaxies? Of course, these questions are unanswerable, but they are important to ask as one approaches the conclusion of a long life. The perspective a man reaches as a result of this long meditation will be an important piece of the heritage he leaves to the generations following. Will he leave behind a sad and embittered image, or will it be a hopeful and encouraging one? Or a balanced one, combining both positive and negative features? For certain, it can't be faked.

The attempt to expand one's consciousness far enough to include all aspects of reality in its multiplicity is the work of finding wholeness. Wholeness is a master term. It refers to reality *per se*, and its symbol is the mandala. Striving for wholeness implies stretching consciousness to include a maximum scope on reality and to see it without distortion, neither rationalizing evil away nor trying to turn it into good, nor cynically turning good into bad. The attempt to stretch consciousness to the point of containing reality as it presents itself in all its aspects is a man's attempt to achieve wholeness. That is the fifth circle.

The struggle with God in old age becomes an internal dialogue. That internal dialogue may externalize itself in certain ways, possibly as teachings or perhaps as writings or verbal statements of wisdom about life. Unfortunately, when old people try to teach the young in inappropriate ways, the young are disinclined to listen. But when they embody wisdom as tribal elders, perhaps they need not say anything further. Rather, they may embody in their being and their actions an achievement of the inner balance among the opposites. In doing so, they can influence those who come in contact with them because they will constellate Self projections even in their silence and will thus function as models. By their simple presence they carry the projections of the wise old man and the Self. For themselves, it is important to have struggled through to some congruence with the Self.

An older person who has done this work will be able to exemplify a radical freedom to be essentially what he is. Older people often observe that after a certain age they no longer have to worry about what others think. It is important, however, to distinguish between being *what* one is and *who* one is. The question of who one is, is an identity problem that is personalistic and egocentric. What one is, is a Self definition. Being what one is, rather than only who one is, presents a much closer approximation to the Self. Such people are not trapped in social role definitions.

This image of the wise old man, or sage, is one that includes potential for further growth, creativity, and wisdom, in contrast to the image of old age as a time of increasing deficits in ability. If taken in the right spirit, such physical deficits can even function as stimulants to another kind of development and as part of the struggle with the Self. The contributions to culture that old people make are unique and special. A culture is blessed if it possesses figures that can carry the projection of the wise old man because they can orient people toward meaning and purpose.

I often think of Jung's biography as an illustration of the struggles that transpire in the fifth circle for a man in his later years. Toward the end of his life, Jung became more and more engaged with two fundamental issues: the problem of evil and the problem of uniting the opposites. He took these up specifically in his late works *Answer to Job* and *Mysterium Coniunctionis*. In the first, he speaks in a very personal voice and with great passion and drama. In the second, his style returns to the usual analytical and interpretive mode. Describing how *Answer to Job* came to be, Jung says he was "gripped by his *daimon*." While recovering from a bout of illness, he wrote feverishly and finally announced to Aniela Jaffé, his secretary, in a letter from his Tower in Bollingen: "I have landed the great fish." The composition of this text was both a personal struggle for Jung with the problem of evil and a message to his contemporaries about the need for further evolution in Western religious history and culture.

In *Answer to Job*, Jung discussed the idea of the evolution of the God image. This evolution comes about as a result of a confrontation between the ego and the Self, or in traditional terms between man and God. It is characteristic that in the last part of life psychology becomes equated with theology. One can no longer keep the strict division between the personal and the theological. As ego and Self merge, ego and transcendent world also become one. Earlier in life, this would result in inflation. Late in life this becomes wisdom.

From our perspective, we see Jung as an old man in the fifth circle in the process of confronting another dimension of life beyond the personal level of ego-consciousness. His aspiration is to advance a collective unconscious-conscious dynamic that reaches far beyond his own individual life and his times. If the individual has evolved far enough, he may gain leverage to move religious tradition and the collective view of God to another level of wholeness.

Jung was also attempting to resolve questions of good and evil in his own life, and he had to deal with the despair of old age. The wells of creativity can dry up in old age, although tremendous amounts of new creativity can also still appear, as they certainly did in Jung's late years. The old person will be dealing with the shadow—his own, his tribe's, his culture's—and can easily become lost in the darkness and fall into despair. Jung also experienced this in his late years. But if he remains engaged in the project of individuation, he will go on to forge what Jung referred to as a *Weltanschauung*, a fundamental attitude toward life flowing from a worldview that includes good and evil and that expresses the whole Self. He becomes a wise old man, the embodiment of an archetype within a cultural context. He performs the role of elder, as is so dramatically seen among non-technological, natural peoples—as one who represents the wisdom of the generations, the tribal gods, and the highest religious values.

As much as he denied it, Jung became an archetypal figure for many people. No longer seen as just a psychologist or philosopher, he elaborated in his writings a gestalt that is a model to which many people have turned for orientation within the modern world.

After *Answer to Job* in approximately 1952, Jung went on to finish the *Mysterium Coniunctionis*, a book on the mysterious union of opposites. This vision of integration of the whole personality is what preoccupied Jung in the last twenty years of his life. It was the symbol that channeled his creative energy, and he became remarkably productive in the final decades of his life, writing major works on topics of major importance for his and our times.

On Friendship Between Men

"When a man becomes dear to me, I have touched the goal of fortune," Emerson writes in his justly famous essay, "Friendship."[3] How many men in their adulthood know this experience? It is my impression, based on personal observation, conversation, clinical experience and on reading journals, magazines, and articles that the number of men who can claim to have deep friendships with other men is statistically tiny. Maybe men just don't know how to do friendship. John Beebe writes movingly of "the presence of an absence" in men's relationships, the absence being competence at intimacy.[4]

For most men in our present postmodern times, a close friendship with another man is but a memory from adolescence when one had a buddy with whom one shared innermost thoughts and feelings, dreams and ambitions, and everyday concerns. Male friendships usually tend to come to a halt

---

[3] Ralph Waldo Emerson. *Essays, First Series* (May 25-1803-April 27, 1882). (Toronto: Diamond Books, 2016), p. 169.
[4] John Beebe, 2006. "The Presence of an Absence: A Review of the film 'Brokeback Mountain,'" *The San Francisco Jung Institute Library Journal*, Vol. 25/1, pp. 78-90.

upon serious engagement with a female partner. From then on, all intimacy flows into this channel, and all confidences are reserved for this relationship. From then on, relations with men are conducted within the contexts of study, work, team projects, and professional associations. This is not to deny their value and even profound sense of loyalty and bonding, but they are not what Emerson had in mind when he spoke the words quoted above.

It's not that relating to a woman is easier than it is to a man, but it is different. Both are complex, but in different ways. And the rewards that come from entering into a personal relationship are also different.

We know well that the psyche needs the world, and most importantly persons in the surrounding world, in order to become fully activated and set on course for optimal development. A psyche without important relations to the world around would be exceedingly barren and would remain stunted, held back in shadowy potential. It is especially close persons in our lives who matter deeply to us and with whom we form emotional bonds that activate the psyche's potential for consciousness and growth. As we project parts of our psyches into and upon objects and persons in the world and receive content back from them through the process called introjection, we activate essential parts of the self. I will try to expand on this in what follows with special attention to men's relationships with other men in the bond that we call friendship.

Think for a moment of the psyche as a round object with a number of sensitive spaces to be activated over a lifetime. Experiences with significant people bring these spaces into play and activate them. The spaces are potential areas of personality development, and through activation they become a part of an individual's complete selfhood. These spaces need to be activated, filled in with specific content, and used. Empty, they remain useless, only potential, and the personality does not become fully manifest.

How many such spaces are there in the psyche? Following Jung, we think of these centers of potential as archetypes, inborn potentials for behavior, perception, and development. So far no one has proven that there is a definite number of them. I prefer to try not to err on the side of too many or too few. If you count too few, you fall into reductionism. If you allow for too many, they lose their psychic significance.

To begin, there are the two Big Ones: Mother and Father. Each of these is activated by the experience of an actual mother and father and then gradually takes the form of an internal psychic representation of a specific type and quality. Partly these are conscious as memory images, and partly they are unconscious as complexes. These embedded memories and complexes remain with us for life and are put to various uses. Then there are the two that I consider to be somewhat related but different enough to count them separately: Sister and Brother. And finally, there are two more that we'll name Lover and Friend.

For a man, Mother, Sister, and Lover lie on a continuum, as do Father, Brother, and Friend. As the boy grows into manhood and matures, these centers become activated and differentiated. The later ones—that is, Sister and Lover—inevitably retain tonal shades of coloration from the earlier ones. Thus, Lover may be similar to Sister who may be similar to Mother. For a grown man, his Beloved is also his soul Sister and his archetypal Mother, as all of this feminine element of his personality finds itself expressed in the person of a SHE. And so also and in parallel, Friend is archetypally continuous with Brother and with Father. When a man "becomes dear," to use Emerson's touching phrase, and becomes a Friend, the psyche is likely to project into this figure its proclivities (and its aversions) to Brother and Father as well.

As a man will inevitably come into contact with his Sister Soul and his Mother Ground in an intense intimate relationship with a woman, so with a male friend he will face his shadow Brother and the spirit of the Father. As the Lover connects a man to his body and his primal instinct of sexuality and channels his capacity for love into the specific and the particular, so the latter connects him to male shadow of aggression and also potentially to spiritual transcendence, ultimately to the possibility for a broadened sense of community. We hear this magnificently intoned in Beethoven's "Ninth Symphony," which gives such powerful emotional expression to the German poet Friedrich Schiller's lines: "*Alle Menschen werden Brüder!*" ("All peoples will become brothers").

It is common knowledge that a man needs a woman for his soul-making. We don't know quite as well that a man needs a man as Friend in order to confront his shadow, to relativize his ego in making room for this brother, and to gain through this process the capacity for community-building. The psychic center that a Lover activates in a man is the anima; the center that a male Friend activates is the shadow. The importance of the latter is vastly underestimated in our culture, which is one reason why it remains so individualistically oriented. If a man does not find a strong and secure bridge to other men through the experience of friendship, he will not be enabled to build community. He will stay at home and isolate himself in the anima world, in a one-sided exclusivity and interiority.

Individuation proceeds in a sort of helix pattern with respect to mother-father, sister-brother, lover-friend constellations and integrations. A fixation on one side of this helix structure will arrest development toward wholeness.

I will now consider three possible types of friendship between men, which are strongly conditioned by how development has gone along on the feminine side of the helix. Of course, there are many variations on each of these three types.

The first is what I will call "in-the-mother friendship," following the nomenclature in the lectures on men's individuation (see lectures above). By this I mean a male-to-male bond that is characterized by psychic fusion between two. In this type, the friendship rests on unconscious identity, which merges the two into one single psychic entity. This serves to fulfill an unconscious longing for paradise, for union with the other, for no differences or boundaries. The two become one. The identity of the one person assumes the identity of the other and this runs in both directions, so it takes on the image of two identical heads on one body. The two men mirror one another. There are no differences in their attitudes toward the world. They unite against others and form an exclusive relationship as a couple. One sees the same in heterosexual couples where man and woman are fused.

This type of relationship occurs when a man's ego has not sufficiently separated from his mother complex, that is, from the unconscious ground out of which it emerges in early childhood. An identity between ego and unconscious ("mother") background remains and affects all other relationships. A relationship between the two men based on this psychic background is largely unconscious. They connect to each other intuitively, often in a quasi-magical way. Words are not needed to express feelings because they are communicated via unconscious channels. The men are largely silent, therefore, but this does not mean that nothing is passing between them. The friendship between the two exists psychologically in the same boundless and diffuse atmosphere that characterizes their ego identities. They are both quite undeveloped and unformed. There is a childish and infantile character about this type of friendship. It is an early version of friendship.

A more advanced type of friendship becomes possible when a man has separated more decisively from his mother complex and his unconscious background and has drawn a distinct line between himself as a man and his latent feminine traits and qualities. In this stage he has identified himself firmly with masculine features of his personality. In other words, he has become a man in a clear and distinct sense. His male relationships now become characterized by competitiveness. Suspicion and even hostility enter into his relations with other men. There are contests of physical prowess and aggressiveness is highly valued. However, certain aspects of his being have been repressed and become lodged in the shadow, which represents "the other." This kind of man greets another with initial suspicion, which triggers a response of anxiety in the other. When these kinds of men do form friendships, the friendship usually begins with a fight. Then, when hostilities cease, they may become fast friends. These are the warriors. Classically, the Babylonian hero

Gilgamesh and his companion Enkidu fit this description. They meet originally at the city gate and engage in a vicious wrestling match, after which they become fast friends and go about performing heroic deeds together. The male friend in this version is a shadow brother. At first a worthy opponent, later a buddy, but always with some measure of inequality between them. It is an ego-shadow relationship. Teenager boys often form this type of bond between themselves.

One of my boyhood heroes was the Lone Ranger. He was invariably accompanied by Tonto, his trusted Indian sidekick. All of their exploits were mutual efforts, and many were the times that they saved each other's lives and together proved themselves up the task of dispensing justice. And yet this figure was known as the *Lone* Ranger. Why "Lone"? Because his friend was a shadow figure and remained without a very distinct history or identity. His personality was dependent on his relationship with the Lone Ranger. Like Enkidu who came from the "beyond," Tonto was of another culture. He was largely unacknowledged and remained in the shadows despite his critical importance in the adventures. How many of our so-called "lone rangers"—those "self-made" men who appear to be so utterly self-sufficient—are secretly and unconsciously dependent on a silent friend, a dutiful organization, or a quietly supportive assistant? These male relationships are hierarchically structured.

The only incident that I clearly remember from years of listening to the Lone Ranger programs on the radio was one when Tonto got into trouble. The bad guys had captured him and tied him to a stake in a canyon and left him to die under the blazing sun. For nights and weeks afterward, I was gripped by the haunting call of Tonto for his friend, echoing through the chambers of the desert canyon: "Kemo Sabe, Kemo Sabe." So poignant, this call for help from the friend in trouble. In the end, the Lone Ranger saved him, to my great relief.

Something in us knows that when the shadow friend dies, something in us also dies. Our lives are irrefrangibly joined to one another. In this type of friendship there is also a remnant of the bond of identity so paramount in the first type. In psychology, we call this projective identification, or *participation mystique*.

There is a third type of male friendship, which I will call the "maturity friendship." This becomes possible when a man has firmly and decisively differentiated his ego from the mother complex (the unconscious) but has also integrated into his ego attitude some of the elements of the shadow and also some of the unconscious feminine aspects of his personality. Earlier I mentioned that the Friend exists on an archetypal continuum with the Brother and the

Father. By this I mean that in a man's friendship with another man to whom he is not related by blood there will be some resonance with the other psychic structures. This means, in practical terms, that the dynamics of male friendship will be fraught to some extent with Oedipal and sibling rivalry dynamics. This introduces the two great impediments to male-to-male friendship between adult men. The first is castration anxiety, and the second is envy.

The adult man's preference for hierarchical relations with other men is rooted in the Oedipal dynamic. For a man who is threatened by serious castration anxiety, the only tolerable relation to another male is a hierarchical one: either above or below is comfortable, but any movement toward altering this structure produces intolerable anxiety. For this kind of a man, friendship with another man of the intimate sort I was describing is not in the cards. This man can accept a master and he can accept a servant, but he cannot relate comfortably to a male equal.

Should a man work through this problem, he may be confronted by another obstacle. This has to do with sibling rivalry. We know these stories well from novels and films, and historically they have been the grist of family narratives since recorded history began. In the Bible, the most infamous murderer is the envious killer of his brother: Cain. Joseph's envious brothers seek to kill him but instead sell him into slavery in Egypt. Fratricide based on sibling rivalry runs through the Bible like a Wagnerian leitmotif. The envy that gets constellated between brothers has its origin in a perception that one is special or gifted in a way that the other is not. One is cleverer (Jacob over Esau), or one's gift is more favored (Abel over Cain), or one is favored by a parent and given special privileges (Joseph over his brother). This sense that the one is chosen over the other erodes the other's self-esteem and ultimately threatens to deprive him of a sense of self-esteem. Left empty and rejected, he retaliates. Envy is a murderous emotion. So, in men where the sense of self is not inwardly well rooted and tends to be measured against the value given to the other by society or important authority figures, the potential for friendship is seriously diminished.

Supposing these drawbacks are not too severe, however, and that shadow integration is sufficient to allow the openness and receptivity needed for intimate friendship, what then?

There are some examples of male friendship to look to as models, but in our culture not many. The author David Michaelis went in search of such friendships and published a book of interviews and descriptions titled *The Best of Friends: Profiles of Extraordinary Friendships*.[5] The book contains an account of seven friendships between men. Among

---

[5] David Michaelis, 1983. *The Best of Friends: Profiles of Men and Friendship* (New York: William Morrow & Co.).

those discussed are two captains of industry (Don Louris of Quaker Oats and George Love, President of Consolidation Coal), inventor/artists (Isamu Noguchi and Buckminster Fuller), entertainers (Dan Ackroyd and John Belushi), adventurers (the mountain climbers Leonard Picotte and Michael Edwards) and the politicians LeMoyne Billings and John Kennedy. These are persons for whom friendship was longstanding in duration and deeply significant. In a review of this book, Jungian psychotherapist Robert Hopcke writes: "These friendships are between men *who act*" and engage in common activities such as "sailing, commerce, designing, roughhousing, mountain climbing, performing comedy, commanding ships, drinking, traveling.... These are not quiet friendships of peaceful moments shared in the lull of the evening, but energetic beings, creating, producing, well within the realm of homo faber...[Their] productivity was both an expression of their maleness and glue for their relationships."[6] Hopcke also notes that these friendships show evidence of the presence of the anima as a function of feelings of deep connectedness and bonding between the friends. It is this combination that deserves the title of friendship.

Speaking again of the helix relationship of masculine and feminine aspects of the personality

---

[6] Robert H. Hopcke, 1987, "Eros in All His Masculinity: Men as Lovers, Men as Friends," *The San Francisco Jung Institute Library Journal*, Vol. 7/4, p. 37.

mentioned above, we can observe that within the unconscious there has been a development on the feminine side such that the anima has evolved out of the maternal ground, has by this point in a man's development been found in projected form in lovers, and has gradually been integrated into ego consciousness through a process of mirroring. When a man has had the good fortune to be in steady and continuous relationship with a beloved who has carried his anima projection well and over a period of time, who has gently and firmly helped him to take responsibility for the projected elements in service of their relationship, this man has within his ego structures some (at least) of the feminine qualities that make depth of intimacy possible. Here there is no "presence of an absence," as spoken about by John Beebe in his review of the film "Brokeback Mountain" cited earlier. Such men know to conduct themselves in an intimate relationship.

Ordinarily, the average man lets his female partner do the feeling, the relating, the tending and attending to the emotional needs of others. The young man sees all of this as not very "manly." But through loving and mirroring and encouragement, as well as through crises and challenges and torment and accusation, a man may develop some of these capacities in himself as well. This is the post-patriarchal man, and it is this man who is able to have and to enjoy friendships with other men in the high and noble sense of friendship that Emerson writes about.

First shadow, then anima integration are the ingredients that make the third type of friendship between men possible. When the masculine shadow is integrated and the door to the anima as an inner function is opened in a man's personality, a capacity for tenderness, for sensitivity to feelings, and for a positive valuation of emotional life for its own sake become possible without losing a sense of manliness or separateness and difference without hostility and competitiveness. Because of shadow integration, the masculine is not swallowed up and dominated by the feminine. Then, a man who has access to the anima as a function of his conscious personality can hold and contain, as well as act and initiate. There is an ability to engage in play with another man without falling into macho competition, even though competition may be part of the play. There is the enjoyment of a lunch that is not a power lunch, but only chatting and exchanging thoughts and feelings for a period of time over food and drink. There is a space for conversation without the requirement of decision and closure. The ego's desire for achievement, for conquest, for surmounting obstacles and climbing every mountain can be put aside for the sake of banter, play, the quiet exchange of views, and for casual reminiscing. This development of the personality makes a more intimate type of friendship possible.

It is well known that many men find it difficult, even painful, trying to talk about personal matters: their marriages, their conflicts, their sexual hang-ups and fantasies. It's not the lack of language that's to blame. It's the inhibitions. Hidden behind these inhibitions are fears of inadequacy, indeed a sense of shame about having any feelings and longings at all. There is anxiety about being bested in the competition for prowess. Mostly when men talk about sex they brag; rarely do they admit failure, inexperience, unfulfilled longing, inadequacy.

My thought is that the post-patriarchal man will do better. The anima offers space for tender feelings. For Emerson, this was one of the two essential ingredients of true friendship, the other being sincerity.[7]

Martin Scorsese's film, "The Last Temptation of Christ," features scenes of friendship between Jesus and Judas that are particularly touching and, in relation to our theme, instructive. They take their cue from the Gospel of John, which of the Gospels shows Jesus at his most intimate with his friends, the disciples. There is one scene in the film that takes place under a tree one night when Jesus can't sleep and is troubled by his doubts. Judas is sitting beside him. At a certain moment Jesus is lying in Judas' arms and Judas is comforting him. Jesus is talking soul talk, the

---

[7] Emerson., pp. 168-69.

kind of talk a man will usually only dare with a sweetheart, a female lover. There is nothing sexual in the feeling of this scene. It is intimate, a man sharing his uncertainty with a friend. For most men, the closest approximation to this comes in analysis after the defenses have been let down, trust has been established, and the male analyst has demonstrated his trustworthiness and his capacity to hold and contain emotion. Then the secret fears can be confessed, the inner life can be revealed, and the real story told.

Emerson concludes his lengthy disquisition on the subtleties, pitfalls, glories, and deceptions of friendship with the stirring line: "The essence of friendship is entireness, a total magnanimity and trust."[8] It is only an entire person who can offer this or accept it. And this is the reason for its rarity among us.

---

[8] Ibid., pp. 179-80.

Gestures of Fathering[9]

One: The Gesture of Choosing

When I started thinking seriously about the topic of fathers and fatherhood, my own father had recently passed away so the issue was personally relevant. In retrospect, I realized what an important figure he had been in my life. He died at the age of 68 of cancer in a hospital in Winnipeg, Manitoba, some 200 miles from where he had engendered me some 38 years earlier. He was a highly regarded and much loved minister in the North American Baptist Church, a small religious denomination with roots in the Swiss and German Anabaptist tradition. My memories of him are many, most of them associated with the church. There is a story that when I was around two years old, I made something of a spectacle of myself in a church service by standing on the pew and "preaching," waving my arms and speaking very loudly in synch with my father up in the pulpit. Another time I was found by my mother preaching to some youngsters from the back

[9] This text is based on a series of lectures I gave at the C.G. Jung Center in Evanston, IL, in 1985. The audience was composed mostly of training candidates at the Chicago Jung Institute. I have edited and modified the original lectures somewhat for this publication.

111

of a truck. My earliest memory, which dates from about the age of 24 months, is of being with my father and playing hide-and-seek with him in a country store. The memory still brings tears to my eyes. I recall the smell and the spirit of him vividly. He was an extraverted people person and in his mature adulthood extremely vital physically. He loved to eat, to tell stories, and laugh. And he was completely given to his vocation as a minister of the gospel. He served the gospel of Jesus Christ with unrestrained zeal and enthusiasm.

My father's role in my life is, of course, not simple. It was through a combination of identification with him, with his mission in life, with his deep-felt beliefs and loves and preferences on the one hand, and a rebellious reaction against him—his paucity of intellectual finesse and the influence on him of his anima moods and predilections—that much of what I am and hold dearly, or also reject, took a specific form. My early memories are of an Eros father; the adolescent memories are of strife and conflict and rupture; and the last memories are of reconciliation as he peacefully slipped away into what he forever longed for, the blessed rest of eternity.

I've asked myself: In all this jumble of memories, what is personal and actually related to the man my father was, and what is archetypal and the product of projections? I have to confess that the Heavenly Father and my dad are mixed together, and my feelings for one slide over into my feeling for the others. In theory, we make such a large distinction between the personal and the impersonal. I've wondered about this distinction a good deal.

As psychoanalysts, we know that in the transference there is usually a personal element that is based on the client's earlier experience of father. The commonly held concept of transference among psychoanalytically trained therapists assumes that the early experience of a parent figure is carried over wholesale and fixed to a stranger, the analyst. However, there is a paradox here. It seems that in a sense the past counts for nothing when transference appears. The amount of experience that went into my father complex—all the years of love and hate and struggle and disappointment and disillusionment and coming to terms with a less than perfect father—were wiped away when I developed a transference to my first therapist. It emerged suddenly and with force from a level of psyche that had very little to do with memory, learning, or personal history. Transference creates a gap in historical continuity. It is not a simple loop back to what once actually was. Freud believed that transference brings about a repetition of a childhood experience of the parent; Jung went deeper and said that the childhood experience was itself shaped by an archetypal structure. Children project the mother and father archetype onto their actual parents and react to this projection as much as or more than they react to the real persons who happen to be their parents. We are structured from the beginning by projection of "father" upon our fathers. The purpose of this is to make them into fathers by responding to our desires and needs for a father. There is in the parent as well as in the child an unconscious mirroring that creates, or as we say "constellates," the desired relationship. Transference does it all over again, and that's how the client turns the analyst into the transference object that is needed.

This to say that it is difficult to tell the difference between my actual father and the father archetype. If the archetype did its work well, it turned my actual father into what he was supposed to be in order to conform to the pattern. So, my father and the deeper pattern are very similar, and history has so intertwined them that I can't tell one from the other. They are wed. Forever the father God will be my father, and my father will be God, because the fit was so close. He did what he was supposed to do. First, he created me, then he loved me, and finally he preferred me over all the other children on Earth. I was created and chosen by him. Later, he also made great demands on me: he expected me to be better than all the other kids (after all, I was the "Preacher's kid"); I was supposed to be an example, a "light to the nations," to be their "priest," as the Bible speaks of the chosen people. And this put a terrible burden on me. I hated it. I rebelled. I ran after other gods (for a long while I attended the other church across town because I like the minister over there much better). My father suffered from this way-wardness, and we fought, we argued, I tried to best him in theology, to know more and know better. And on his deathbed we were reconciled, as in "by His death we are healed." Atonement, reconciliation, peace between him and me came about in the end. And now I feel very strongly that he is in heaven, that he is sitting up there at the right hand or in the big chair himself, at least preaching somewhere to somebody up there... The whole biblical myth lives in my psyche. I am convinced that when I die and go to heaven and see God face-to-face face, I will find myself looking into my father's face.

This is how archetypes work. They create a field of responsiveness in which the first person ("I") is one essential ingredient, and the second ("you") is the other essential ingredient. This field affects both and induces certain feelings, behavior patterns, and typical responses. A carefully patterned relationship is created. The underlying archetype influences and changes them both. The father archetype constellates a field in which one person becomes the son and the other the father.

What we want to consider here are certain features in the archetypal pattern of fathering. We want to study the psychology of this archetypal pattern.

I make a distinction between archetypal images on the one hand and archetypal actions and gestures

on the other. By "gestures of fathering," I mean everything from body language to enacted attitudes and
all the ways of tailoring behavior and communication
and interaction along the lines that we call "fathering."
One experiences fathering and being fathered in
"gestures" before one has an image of it. An image of
a father figure in myth, like Zeus or Yahweh, is a filled-
out portrait with certain specific and characteristic
features. These images contain something of the
archetype in their features, but there is also much
that is cultural and worked over through a period of
history that goes into the creation of an image. A father
image is elaborated over time. It comes later developmentally than the elemental gestures and captures the
"fathering gestures" that precede it. In other words,
experience precedes imagination. Imagination captures unconscious experience and makes it visible.

Fathering comes about through the constellation of a highly emotional bond between a man
and his child. This bond is irrational in the sense that it
might not make sense in practical or obviously realistic
terms. It either happens or it doesn't happen, and the
cause is opaque, even mysterious. Fathers choose their
children, and they do it irrationally. This choice is not
based on considerations of looks or talent or birth
order. It may be based on smell or some kind of
invisible affinity. But this is hard to pin down. It is a
mystery. The father is also chosen by the archetype.
Some children in a family are more strongly chosen

than others even if all are loved and cared for. The one favored will always know it, as will the ones who are not. Others will know it too, because it shows itself in many derivative gestures. Contrary gestures— rejecting, slighting, turning away, preferring someone else—are not the negative side of fathering; they indicate the absence of fathering. Rejection, disinterest and neutrality do not belong essentially to fathering. Fathering is passionate, it is irrational, and one of its key features is choosing and being chosen.

When this happens between two persons, it signifies "destiny." When father says you're chosen, you are forever marked. And so is he. It is a common destiny. This bond creates and ensures a future. It brings relational cohesion and loyalty and love and struggle that continue in the history of families and tribes. If we plumb the depths of fathering to the archetypal level, the gesture we most characteristically find is one that says: "I chose you; you're my favorite; more than all the others, I favor you." To be recognized in this way is what it means to have a father. The absence of this experience is evident in all of our therapy practices, in the insatiable quest of our patients to find a father practically by any means available. It is also evident in culture and society. For a man, being chosen by his father creates the difference between being included and excluded, between finding commitment and drifting. The foundational basis of fathering is the gesture of choosing, an irrational, passionate, exclusive choice.

How is this different from the archetypal gesture of mothering? The difference lies not in one being more basic or more profound than the other. Rather, it stems from the fact that mothering begins by first carrying children within the body, whereas fathers first experience children as "other." Fathering gestures occur after birth, or later in childhood. The essential gesture of "mothering" is much closer to an act of self-love than an act of other-love. Thus, it is not a gesture of choosing one from among others. It is *self-affirmation*. A mother makes her essential gesture by affirming her own being, part of which has now budded off in the form of a child. A mother's love is therefore much more like fusion, close intimacy, and identification, while a father's love recognizes sepa-rateness and consists of a bond between two individuals.

Two: The Gestures of Law-Giving and Law-Maintaining

In the previous section I focused on "choosing" as an elemental gesture of fathering. To be chosen by a father is to be preferred by him above others, especially above non-tribal outsiders and non-family children. Within families, too, there is preference and status. Some children are preferred above the others even though the father may be quite even-handed and does not intend to show such preference. Almost inevitably, some children will feel slighted by favor shown to the special one, and much of sibling rivalry springs from this perception. The biblical story of Joseph and his brothers is a classic example. Although Jacob loved all the children, only Joseph received a coat of many colors. Thereafter his brothers looked on him as special and preferred in the eyes of their father. Joseph was the youngest of the brothers, and his privileged position created a certain amount of inflation and led him to boast and not consider his brothers' feelings. This in turn led to their attempt to expunge his presence from the family. Currents of envy and hatred inevitably swirl around the father-child bond of privilege.

In this lecture, I will consider a second elemental gesture of fathering: law-giving and law-maintaining. The father is the source of explicit law, archetypally speaking. He is a lawgiver. There is also, of course, mother-law, which is a kind of tacit under-standing of primal values whereas father-law is explicit and spelled out in clear commandments and written documents. Father-law is not something you have to guess about or intuit. You can look up the rules in books and codes.

Archetypal images, such as the great mytho-logical figures that we know as Father Gods, contain a conglomeration of a number of elemental gestures that have been codified and shaped into specific forms. The gestures themselves, however, are more elementary. They are involuntary expressions of instinct like blinking the eyes when something threatens to hit them. They are reflex reactions, basic patterns of behavior. Fathers can't help preferring their children over the neighbors' children or laying down rules and laws, and, as with all instinctual impulses, after a certain point one doesn't want to stop them. The fathering gesture of law-giving is like this. Fathers do it because it belongs fundamentally to the pattern of fathering. It is instinctual. Fathers create boundaries and demand obedience. More than that, in later stages of development they include the element of objectivity: laws are to be obeyed for their own sake and not just to please the father. Obedience to the law is a value in its own right no matter if anyone is around to observe or enforce or praise such acts of obedience. It becomes a matter of conscience and integrity. Logos is called into play. And this leads to ethics as a rational act of discrimination and choice among possible actions and to a type of conscience that transcends the culture's legal system.

When we take up the theme of conscience in psychology, what quickly comes to mind is Freud's theory of the superego. When Freud created his psychological typography and divided the mental cosmos into three parts—id, ego, and superego—he was addressing the issues of law versus impulsivity and culture versus nature. The id is raw instinctual nature, the superego is father's law enforced by his will, and the ego must navigate between these two awesome powers. Jung commented about the superego that it was Freud's way of inscribing Yahweh into his psychological theory. Yahweh is the biblical lawgiver who inscribes his rules in stone and asks his prophet, Moses, to impose them on the unruly chosen people. The superego is the psychological agency that stands for law against impulsive instinctual gratification, the incest wish, debauchery, and rampant sexuality. The superego is an inner spokesman for the father's law. It is the agency that keeps us from becoming lawless when we are no longer under the direct supervision of the father. Freud understood the superego as coming into being as the result of the Oedipal struggle with the father. As an image of the castration-threatening father, the superego demands the allegiance of the ego against the persuasions of the id and threatens violent punishment if this is not acknowledged. While the law originated with the father, it ended up deeply embedded in the son's inner world. This conflict between law and instinct and the strategies used by the ego to resolve it and to gain some measure of instinctual gratification, albeit in sublimated form, produce both civilization and its discontents.

According to Freud's theory, the role of the father in the life of the child is to bring about the creation of the superego. However, the superego is not simply the internalized father image, so its existence is not dependent on the father's presence or absence in the life of the young son. The superego is often much harsher and more demanding than the actual father ever was. The superego is "constellated" by the father, as it were, and is not simply an inner representative of his actual reality. Its source of energy is in the unconscious, in the "drive" that Freud named Thanatos, the death wish, which stands over against Eros, the life wish. The truest image of the superego is not the personal father, therefore, but rather something like a Hades figure or an inner demonic death-dealer. It is through the law-giving gesture of the father that this agent is constellated and comes into place in the inner world of the individual. The father's threatening gesture calls it forth.

Jung had quite a different opinion on the question of the origins and purpose of conscience. For Jung, the law is written in the psyche at an archetypal level from the beginning of life. The role of the father, by his gesture of law-giving, is to call it into being in a person's life. At a first level, the father with his laws reinforces the pressure to conform to family mores and cultural norms. A young, undeveloped ego will feel this pressure as tyrannous and brutal. This is the "terrible father" period. A later and more mature ego will still feel these pressures but be able to resist them or put them in perspective. Persona pressure, which is the urge to conform to social norms, does have a source in the depths of the psyche, since persona adaptation is part of the individual's survival capacity and is therefore archetypally rooted. The mirror neurons play a part, so it begins very early. At an early stage of ego development, such as that of the four-year-old child, Jung would have agreed with Freud that the "castrating father" and the sense of moral duty and the fear of death could well come together and be represented in a death-dealing Father figure. And in regressed ego states in adulthood, which come about in crisis situations, this can again be the case. But what conscience is later, for the integrated, high-functioning, individuating person, is a very different thing. Here we may speak of a sense of law written within the self and of individual conscience as the voice of the Self.

Developmentally, the locus of the lawgiver is first "out there" in the parental figure, the father; then one finds it "in there," as superego, a representative of collective values and driven by destructive urgency and anxiety; and finally, we discover conscience in the "objective psyche" as the voice of the Self, again a non-ego agency but one that is not confined to the collective demands and expectations of society, family, or culture.

The elemental gesture of law-giving in the archetypal pattern of fathering is amplified and made effective by the massiveness of parental power. A parent has this huge amount of power not only by virtue of size and age but also because it is granted through the archetypal transference a child makes to the parent. The child and the parent are circumscribed by an archetypal field, and the parent is as much controlled by this field as the child. The father figure is an *"imago"* that is charged with a dynamism that we cannot attribute to an individual human being. The power of the archetype is not controlled by our conscious egos. We are its servants and at its mercy to an unsuspected degree. A danger is that one may form an unconscious identity with the archetype. The more a father identifies with the archetype, the more unconscious and irresponsible, indeed psychotic, both he and his child will be.

Both fathers and their children are governed by the power of the archetype, both can identify with it, and both can become "psychotic" because of this identification and can enact its elementary gestures. To some extent, however, this is exactly what is humanly necessary: children *need* fathers, and fathers *need* children. Children need fathers to claim them; fathers need children to lay claim to. When the archetype is constellated and claims them, fathers are drawn into becoming lawmakers and children become contained in these laws. It is a mutual provocation, and in it we can find the elementary features of fathering.

One of the unique features of being human is the near absence of instinctual controls on behavior.

Instead of tight instinctual controls that rigidly direct behavior, humans have culture. What evolution has robbed us of in the way of absolute instinctual knowledge about how to behave in given situations or in life generally, it has given back in the capacity to learn. But this freedom from bondage to instinct also creates the particularly human existential problem of choice. Our behavior, our attitudes, and our responses have to be structured through learning experiences; we have to be told what to do, what to look for, and what to like and dislike to an amazingly large extent. As animals, we're not very well wired. The wiring is done later and otherwise. Jung said somewhere that animals are naturally pious; they naturally and automatically follow the law of their natures. Lions hunt and kill game; cats chase mice; birds hunt and build nests. But a man has to *learn* piety.

Enter the father. Nature has devised fathers to replace missing instincts. Fathers therefore have to teach, to guide, and to make a pathway along the unstructured synapses. The presence of a child provokes the father into doing, into becoming a lawgiver and therefore into a creator of culture. The law itself becomes a teacher, a guardian, and a guide for human values and behaviors. The law fills in for the missing instincts. The law is given and backed up by the father, and it is an elemental gesture of fathering to lay down the law and to insist on its maintenance, even when the law runs against self-interest and even sometimes when the law runs counter to his irrational bond to his child.

A man who is psychotic in his fathering, irrationally and totally possessed by the claims of this archetype upon his ego, will inflict the law upon his children with the full force of his position *for their own good*; and psychotically possessed children will respond to this gesture as though it were given by God. They will relish the laying down of law and its rude enforcement as gestures of fathering and caring. This act of dutiful submission to the will of the Father is what it means humanly to be *pious*. "Dutiful to one's gods and one's parents" is what Partridge's *Origins* says of the Italic root of this word "pious." In ancient Italy we know that piety was a matter of life and death, for the paterfamilias could exact capital punishment on his children if they disobeyed his will.

The law stands in the place of the father's will when the father is not present. When a man makes the fathering gesture of lawmaking, he is expressing his will. In the positive sense, the law he lays down serves to function as a guideline for conduct and as an educational tool; in the negative sense, it becomes the tyranny of the father's will over his children, obliging them to obey his will rather than expanding their own wills. The law cuts both ways, making human social functioning possible and infringing upon human freedom and autonomy. The father's law is both a protector and guide and also a taskmaster and tyrant.

When the law-giving of the father turns negative, becomes rigid and destructive, and is perceived only as willfulness and power-mongering, this gesture will be strongly resisted and fought by the healthy person. The struggle between the puer and the senex fires up, for now the father and his son have entered the arena of a struggle for the spirit.

A great deal has been written about the puer-senex struggle. I wrote about it myself in a paper titled "The Devouring Father," where I described some of the gross and more subtle ways in which the spirit of the father captivates and subverts the autonomous spirit of the child and stunts the growth of a personal acquisition of conscience as the voice of the Self. Ouranos, Kronos, and Zeus all demonstrate the father's anxiety about the power of their sons, and each of them tries to use his force to prevent or put off the inevitable revolution. It is inscribed in the basic archetypal pattern that sons outstrip and overcome their fathers, even sharpening their knives on their fathers' swords. This struggle has many levels, ranging from the physical to the spiritual. And perhaps the ultimate challenge is to the father's law and to the rule of law itself. When Jesus challenged the finality of the Mosaic law and all of its legalistic ramifications, it was the ultimate gesture of the puer son freeing himself from the dominance of the senex father, and through this revolution establishing the individual's conscience as the ultimate arbiter of conduct. "The Sabbath was made for man, not man for the Sabbath" is a way of saying: "the father was made for the son, not the son for the father." A father's usefulness is outgrown by his children, as humans have outgrown their need for instinct, and every father at some level senses the threat that he will become superfluous.

To look for a moment beyond the overthrow of the father's law and authority and position, consider the aged Titan, Saturn, who mellowed and developed beyond his demise into the Wise Old Man of the West. There is a state of fathering beyond the gesture of law-giving, and this requires penetrating beyond the laws of culture and society to the inner law that governs the heart and soul. In Jung's understanding, wisdom is to discover the fundamental pathways of the archetypal patterns and to make the mind more and more conform to those. Saturn, the aged and overthrown Father, develops further by submitting to the higher laws of Divinity, and in this manner he comes to represent the Law beyond the laws. This is how the wise old man becomes the image of the Self and continues in a sense the law-making gesture of fathering. His life, his attitude, and his mindfulness become iconic.

Perhaps we can make a rough division of phases in the history of fathers and children into three: the earliest and first, where the fathering gesture of law-giving is met by childlike trust and obedience, an elemental response on the part of the child that "knows" it needs the guidelines of the law because of the absence of instinctual guides; the middle phase of struggle and questioning, of overthrow and revolution, of senex-puer conflict and the offspring's reach for autonomy and personal conscience; and a final phase of reconciliation and reverence for ancestral wisdom, in which the father's law and will are no longer personalized but become archetypal.

Each of these phases is important in its specific way, and a father can do well or poorly in several different ways. We need to develop for fathering an equivalent to D.W. Winnicott's notion of "good enough mothering." Good enough fathering would avoid the pitfall of perfectionism but would insist upon the fundamental gestures being made in a timely and phase-appropriate way. The gesture of preferring and choosing is fundamental to good enough fathering, and it lays the groundwork for a strong emotional relationship between father and child. The father can fail here by refusing the bond or by abusing the power it gives him. The body organ associated with this gesture is the heart. The gesture of law-giving is equally fundamental but comes later. This gesture creates the context of protection of offspring, of teaching them and guiding them in the ways of culture, of facilitating their entry into the greater social world. Here, the gesture of fathering becomes a bridge out of the family nest. Fathers can fall short here in two basic ways: either they personalize the law too much and make it synonymous with their personal wills and thereby create power conflicts, or they renege and absent themselves, thereby leaving a vacuum in the family and consequently in the behavioral repertoire of their children (they have no bridge out and are therefore "on their own" to a large degree). Good enough fathering with respect to this gesture of law-giving lies between these extremes: making the gesture but not too personalized and not too severe, and allowing space for autonomy within basic, firmly upheld rules for living.

Three: The Gesture of Creating

In the elemental gestures of choosing and law-giving, we see the fathering actions of love and command. I want to turn our attention now to the action of generation, the fathering gesture we can refer to as "creating." If, in developmental terms, the gesture of choosing normally attends the father's first glimpse and bonding response to his offspring, and the gesture of law-giving attends the later phases of structuring the growing child, the gesture of creating precedes both, in the original act of coitus between mother and father. Here I want to consider this act of coitus not in terms of pleasure and sexual release or of erotic coupling but as a gesture of primordial fathering.

All of the great father gods are enormously generative and creative. The chosen children of Yahweh will be as numerous as the sands of the sea, we are told; the offspring of Zeus are many. Other mythologies similarly stress the creative gestures of the father gods. Out of the father pour streams of semen like the rains, fertilizing the earth and making it productive. We know of the fate of kings in ancient times whose lands became dry and infertile. Frazier in his *Golden Bough* has documented the rites of exit performed on these hapless leaders when a time of drought fell upon their lands. An infertile father cannot sustain the faith of his family in times of trouble and hardship. In his fertility we see his potency, and it is this potency that attracts the projections he needs to maintain his position of supremacy.

Recall Jung's early childhood dream of the underground phallus. The boy entered an underground room and there discovered behind a green curtain an enormous phallus. It was like a tree trunk, twelve feet high and two feet thick. It was of flesh and at the top, on its head, had a single eye that gazed steadily upward.

> Above the head, however, was an aura of brightness. The thing did not move, yet I had the feeling that it might at any moment crawl off the throne like a worm and creep toward me. I was paralyzed with terror. At that moment I

heard from outside and above me my mother's voice. She called out, "Yes, just look at him. That is the man-eater!" That intensified my terror still more, and I awoke sweating and scared to death.[10]

Aniela Jaffe, in her classic paper, "The Creative Phases of Jung's Life," lays particular emphasis on the importance of this dream of Jung's early childhood. She sees it as his first awareness of his creative daimon, a force that would erupt powerfully throughout his life with creative ideas and visions. We can also recognize in this archetypal dream figure the image of the father god's phallus, his generative power.

The underground phallus is dangerous: "That is the man-eater," his mother says in the dream. The phallus is not only a man-maker, but it can be a man-eater, a *devouring* father. In the psychological sense, being eaten up by the phallus would mean becoming identified with the numinous power it represents. This would instill a state of inflation through identification with potent contents of thought and feeling. In Jung's life this was a more or less continuous danger. Because he was so close to the unconscious and its creative energies, he was occasionally overwhelmed with daimonic creativity. This was, he said, both a curse and a blessing. The daimon would erupt in such episodes as the composition of *Answer to Job*, which Jung says

---

[10] C.G. Jung, Memories, Dreams, Reflections, p. xxx

he wrote at a feverish state over the course of a few days while convalescing from an illness.

Images of impersonal generativity by the father gods are common in mythology. Danae, the mother of Perseus, for example, is impregnated by Zeus in the form of a shower of gold; the Virgin Mary's womb is invisibly stirred to life by the Holy Ghost, an aspect of the invisible father God; Leda was taken by Zeus who came to her in the form of a swan, and Europa by the father god in the form of a bull.

The elemental gesture of fathering that we are considering here, that is, procreating, comes in a variety of images ranging from the primal scene of parental coitus to the subtleties of spiritual inspiration.

We are generally so accustomed to thinking of sex as a means of intense pleasure or as an act of intimate mating and bonding that we neglect another equally important feature of the act of intercourse: procreating. This may seem like a rather passé idea: the purpose of sex is to make children, to bring souls into the world. Biologically considered, though, this is the most correct explanation for the existence of sex in nature. Nature didn't give us sex to have fun with; we have fun with sex so we'll be motivated to create babies. Many men are tricked by nature into becoming fathers when that may be the last thing on their minds while enjoying the pleasure of their sexuality. However it may give a man a feeling of pride and accomplishment to proclaim: "I have fathered a child!"

Some will take pride in hearing their friends say: "He has fathered a large family." At the beginning of a love relationship there is often talk about a woman giving a man a baby, or of him giving her his children. This fantasy between lovers of making children serves to prepare them for their future parenthood. The gesture of fathering begins in a fantasy and through this gesture the gene line is carried on. Fathering begins, as we see, before there are children. There is a *fantasy* of children, but as yet no actual ones. It is this fantasy of children that stimulates the fathering gesture of creating, the fantasy of generations to follow, of fatherhood to a tribe, a clan, a kingdom. To the man in the fathering mode, the act of abortion is anathema, because it defeats his gesture.

Four: The Gestures of Providing, Protecting, Bridging, Sacrificing

I want to remind you of the gestures we have been discussing so far and also of the reasons I am using this term, "gesture." I began by saying that when we discuss the psychology of archetypes we are speaking of elemental psychic facts and patterns. I believe these elemental facts emerge first at the level of body and action before they permeate consciousness as image. The archetypal image is a secondary product and as such either leaves out portions of the archetype per se or contaminates what we might think of as pure archetypal form with a cultural and personal admixture. Jung thought of the archetype as a type of Kantian *Ding an sich*, a reality that we could not experience or perceive or conceive, directly similar to God. I have taken the approach that we might get closer to it by observing basic human gestures, in this case those we can speak of and label as fathering gestures. No doubt my conception of these gestures is also contaminated by my personal experience and by cultural habits and forms. Nevertheless I will proceed on the assumption that what is limited by culture and personal spheres of influence can be sorted out later through comparisons with other cultures and other persons' experiences of fathering. In theory, the archetypes are a part of the basic human endowment, and as such, related to what Jung also spoke of as instincts. As I said in an earlier lecture, the instincts in the human being are not very precise. What nature provides other species with in the way of instinctual cues and pathways for appropriate behavior, culture provides humans. Thus, parenting becomes such a complex and educational function in the human species. It would be a mistake, however, to remove ourselves altogether from the notion that instincts do exist and that they play a part in human functioning. It is just that the instincts manifest themselves in humans in an indefinite and obscure way, and so it is necessary to pay careful attention to the levels of human functioning.

We can think, therefore, of a *level* that is archetypal-instinctual but that is surrounded by or covered over with cultural and personal layers. What I am trying to do in speaking of the gestures of fathering is to dig down through the levels to the bits and pieces of this human activity called fathering to consider the elemental, instinctive fragments out of which individuals piece together their own styles of fathering.

We might ask: what is the practical use of doing this, of trying to discern the levels of one or another aspect of human behavior? While this may be considered an end in itself, like becoming conscious, there may be a more practical end. The practical value of knowing about the archetypal patterns is to obtain guidance for becoming more truly who and what we basically are, for living a more authentic life as a human being. Nature can assist us by offsetting the one-sided imperatives of culture. Nature does have something normative to say about human behavior. All cannot be left to education and culture. Nature puts limits on culture, even though it allows room for conscious choice and the consequent evolution of culture. But an archetypal psychology, or better said, a psychology of archetypes, is a call back to essentials, to nature and to the basic ground rules of normative human functioning.

It is perhaps one of nature's ironies that once we have removed ourselves from the grip of archetypal patterns and instincts and have appropriated the rights and prerogatives of human freedom, and have thereby granted culture a large measure of authority and freedom over nature, the only way back to know-ledge of the archetypal base is through conscious appropriation and re-education. We are forced to return to nature through the channels provided by culture. This return to nature is what I understand by Paul Ricoeur's "second naiveté." It is this way back to nature that Jung, in his psychology of archetypes, offers to alienated modern women and men.

My argument has been that fathering has an elemental ground plan rooted in an archetypal pattern, and that we can discern this elemental form in the various gestures proper to or characteristic of fathering. I associate each of these gestures with body and physical acts. This is necessary in order to return fathering to the instinctual base out of which it must have originated. I spoke first of the gesture of choosing, by which a father bonds to his child, often a favorite child. A father instinctively prefers his own children above others. This is his heart. The favored child responds with devotion and love for the father. The second gesture I spoke of was law-giving and law-maintaining, by which a father provides structure and behavioral form for his offspring. With this gesture a father uses his physical, moral, and spiritual authority over his children to establish cultural coherence. This is his head. The child responds to this gesture with obedience. The third gesture discussed was creation. The father is a creator and is thus to be located at the origin of life. This is his phallus. With this gesture a father begins things, both biologically and also psychologically by generating movement, activity, and expansion. The children respond with admiration and seek to imitate the father's creativity in their own individual lives.

In this final session I want to refer to a series of four related gestures, which, I believe, are also aspects of the core process in the archetype of fathering. This series runs as follows: providing, protecting, bridging, and sacrificing. The body part associated with these gestures is the hand.

The complex gesture I am now describing as four discrete instances came together in an action of my father's when I was about four years old. My father was an avid gardener, and that year, his harvest outstripped our needs by a considerable amount. I helped him in the garden, proudly pulling my red wagon through the rows of vegetables and gathering up the produce in it. At one point, he told me that if I pulled my wagon along the sidewalk of our small town to the local grocery store, I could perhaps sell the vegetables and make some money. So, I set off in that direction and while I was pulling my loaded wagon down the street with great anticipation, he telephoned the grocer and arranged for him to buy them from me. I came home elated and showed him the money I had received in payment. The following day, he took me to the bank and we opened a savings account. This was my introduction to entrepreneurship and investing.

In this action of his, I can discriminate the series of four gestures I am speaking of: he *provided* (the vegetables, the ideas, the know-how); he *protected* (by telephoning ahead, by ensuring success on this first time out on my own); he *bridged* (out into the world, out of the home into the wider marketplace); and he *sacrificed* (by giving up the profits himself—in fact he had to pay the grocer! and, more importantly, by letting me go off on my own and not coming along). The intended purpose of this complex action is to build up the child's sense of autonomy and confident functioning in the world. In this way the father helps his children bridge out of the sheltered and enclosed world of the mother into the father's world of risk and exploration.

First, we find the gesture of providing. Providing belongs to parenting, and mother and father may divide the chores along the lines of cultural habit or private agreement, but both are committed to the activity. Think of the behavior of other creatures, of birds for instance. The male's gestures of providing begin during the period of incubating the eggs—in human terms, pregnancy. The male gathers provisions for the household when the female is unable to do this.

When the young are born, the male fetches food for the entire family. Similarly, in the human species, the female's pregnancy sets off a response in the fathering male that points him in the direction of providing the necessities of life. If the male is healthy and has separated sufficiently from his mother, he will not identify with the pregnant female by also becoming physically weakened and unable to function, but rather will be activated and engage in the function of providing. He will become a kind of parenting presence to his pregnant spouse, providing her with satisfactions for her oral cravings, with comfort and security, and with emotional support and stability. As the fathering archetype is constellated, the man will measure himself by his ability to provide these necessities for his spouse and family. A proud father is one who has been able to provide adequately for the needs of his family.

The fathering urge to provide can and often does assume pathological overdevelopment in men. Their concept of self-worth becomes totally assimilated to the fantasy of providing for their children, to the extent that they completely lose perspective on what their children actually need. Millions of dollars are left in trust funds for children who are entirely capable of earning their own livelihoods, or would be were it not for the trust funds. These "trusts" serve to satisfy the father's need for making the gesture of providing for his offspring more than they serve their children's needs for provision. The gesture of providing is not brought adequately into contact with the other three gestures that belong to this cluster.

The second is protecting. I am placing this in the second position, but not because it lacks priority. Protecting the young is a gesture often attributed to mothers more than to fathers, as we see, for instance, in the case of the female bear protecting her cubs. In the human realm, this gesture is powerfully constellated in the male when his family and his offspring are threatened. Typically, it is men who defend a tribe's or a nation's territory. In ancient times the military heroes made up the noble class and were honored among the fathers of the nation. George Washington is such a figure in American history. A military hero, he is titled as "the father of his country."

Human parents protect their young instinctively, and this is no less true of fathers than it is of mothers. This protective behavior and attitude is constellated in a man when his family looks to him for it. This is in part what a young man may find himself resisting when he feels the burden of responsibility that is implied in taking a wife and founding a family. The male is expected to fend for his family in the dangerous world of mortgage payments and taxes, and we consider a father adequate only if he does indeed offer protection for his family from the financial and social vicissitudes of life.

It is the combination of these two gestures—providing and protecting—that goes into creating the structures of the "patriarchy." In the patriarchate, the father holds the position of dominance within the family, and his gestures of providing and protecting are highlighted over and above similar gestures of the mother. Provision for daily life and safety in the world depend upon the strength of the father's arm, and it becomes the duty of wife and children to help him maintain his vigor and strength, since the well-being of all depends upon him. Within a social order of this kind, it is incumbent upon a man to make these gestures of providing and protecting to the best of his ability. He has little choice but to do so if he wishes to hold a position of respect within the social order. In these circumstances, a man is seen as mature only when he has achieved the status of householder and head of a family. His gestures of providing and protecting are signals of his maturity as a man. It is inconceivable, in patriarchal terms, for a man to mature adequately in life without a family to provide for and protect.

The next two gesture in this series that I am going to speak of now run, in a way, contrary to those I have just described. Bridging and sacrificing can be seen as running contrary to providing and protecting. Providing and protecting, when taken to the extreme, serve to enclose children within the household's walls, giving them the sense that without papa they cannot survive in the world. They will be hungry and exposed to attack if he is not there at his post. This sense of dependency on the father forms the framework for the psychological imprisonment in the patriarchate. Such radical reliance on the father's perceived power and circle of influence imprisons his children and holds them captive. Some fathers, of course, desire this. Bridging and sacrificing offset this paternalistic effect and form a continuum that completes those two gestures and represents their meaning. These four gestures are four moments or points along a single line of good-enough fathering.

Bridging provides access to the public world outside of the family where business, religion and politics take place. In the early phases of life, providing means feeding and nurturing, and this the father does not do directly with a breast as a mother does but in many indirect ways: by bringing home the bacon, by helping with the baby's feed, and by cuddling and playing. These are tasks the father performs in the first stage of his child's life. The earliest memory of one of my analysands, a woman in her early thirties at the time, was of falling asleep on her father's chest while he was stretched out on the living room floor. Her head was nestled into his strong neck. This presence of the father within the heart of family life later gives way to the child's sense of him as the one who goes out and comes back, bringing the scent of the outer world back into the home with him. And it is because he has been out and come back safely that it is possible for his children to follow, secure in the feeling that the bridge back to home and mother is safe. Without this bridge, the outside world is too fraught with danger to enter, and children will not venture to leave the nest.

One of the problems that can develop in our times, because of the nature of the distance between the work world and home world, is that father is *so* far out in the world that he does not mediate it to the world of home and children. If father goes off early, returns late, works on weekends, travels on business, and works in an environment that is totally and completely foreign and *terra incognita* to the family, the children have no bridge to the outside world that he inhabits. His position in the world is radically split off from his role at home and in the family. The bridging figures then may be schoolteachers, with the result that the children may aspire to become teachers because that is the outer world they know about. School, however, is more or less an extension of family, and the "real world" out there remains a hostile enigma. The father who belongs to that world is also a puzzling, foreign presence, anonymous to his family and unable, even if he wants to, to make the bridging gesture for his children.

Assuming the bridging gesture is made and works, there is still one final gesture of fathering: sacrificing. We might think of this as a gesture of farewell. I think of my father who sent me to the grocer, and I see him standing in front of our large white house watching me pull my red wagon loaded with vegetables down the street and out of sight. I think now: how wise of him not to come along. But I realize as well how hard it must have been for him *not* to come along and to let me meet the unknown other by myself. But the child must meet the stranger, and he or she must deal with the stranger and with the strangeness of life without the continuous, watchful, protective presence of father. In this gesture of letting the child meet reality on his or her own, the father sacrifices his patriarchal hold. Like Moses watching the children of Israel cross Jordan and wind their way into the threat and the promise of a new land, the father must release his children to life and to their own fates. So completely does this fly in the face of the gestures he has made earlier—choosing, law-giving, creating, providing, protecting, bridging—that it can be thought of as an *opus contra naturam*. At this moment the father sacrifices his paternal interests for the sake of the separate well-being of his children.

Obviously, timing is all. And this gesture, like all of the others, must take place in many small ways throughout the fathering process. It would not be good enough fathering to cut his children off suddenly, precipitously, without preparation and warning, just because now they were "old enough" to fend for themselves. They must be able to fly before he pushes them out of the nest. And they must have been able to fly in many small ways before they make the big flight to full independence. The process of releasing children to life and to their own fate begins in tiny ways in infancy and continues through childhood and adolescence. If a father interferes and does a task for a child who can do a it for himself or herself, he is blocking their individuation. On the other hand, if a father fails to make the supportive gestures of fathering when a child cannot perform a necessary task alone, no matter what that child's age or level of development, that also undermines individuation. A sense of timing and understanding the abilities of the child and the size and difficulty of the life task are required of the father who is prepared to make the gesture of sacrificing.

I will always be grateful that my father allowed me to face the grocer by myself.

www.ingramcontent.com/pod-product-compliance
Lightning Source LLC
Chambersburg PA
CBHW020706270326
41928CB00005B/298